Praise for *The Daily Tao*

Filled with inspiration, keen insight, and the ancient wisdom of the *Tao Te Ching*, William Martin's *The Daily Tao* is a vital guide for today's turbulent times. As a wise companion on life's journey, this book invites you to look beyond the busy surface of your days in moments of reflection that can bring you greater awareness, understanding, and peace of mind.

—Diane Dreher, author of *The Tao of Inner Peace*

In *The Daily Tao*, William Martin invites us to join him in walking day by day along the path of the *Tao Te Ching*. As we take each of his 365 steps we feel the presence of a friendly companion at our side. The path is neither straight nor easy, and each one of us treads it in our own unique way—but that doesn't mean we are alone. Drawing skillfully from the timeless wisdom of the *Tao Te Ching*, William Martin gently reminds us how to let go of ourselves and respond instead to the Tao. As he says, "The only step necessary on this walk with the Tao is the one before you at this moment." *The Daily Tao* shows us how to take this step every day.

—Francis Pring-Mill, author of *In Harmony with the Tao: A Guided Journey into the Tao Te Ching* and *There Is No Somewhere Else: Insights from the Tao Te Ching*

William Martin's contemporary rendering of the *Tao Te Ching*'s message is a welcome teaching in these troubled times. His words are simple yet profound, and they provide essential guidance for the major tasks of becoming a wise elder. The wisdom is timeless, the prose is lyrical, and his meditations produce a harmonious resonance for the soul on its journey home in the autumn and winter of life. Simple. Delightful. Inspirational.

—Maggie Meigs, PhD, Director, Forest Dwelling
Program: Spirituality for Our Wisdom Years,
Oblate School of Theology

THE DAILY TAO

Also by William Martin

The Parent's Tao Te Ching

The Couple's Tao Te Ching

The Sage's Tao Te Ching

A Path and a Practice

The Tao of Forgiveness

The Caregiver's Tao Te Ching

The Activist's Tao Te Ching

THE DAILY TAO

365 MEDITATIONS ON THE TAO TE CHING

WILLIAM MARTIN

New York

Hachette Go, an imprint of Hachette Books

Hachette Book Group
1290 Avenue of the Americas
New York, NY 10104
HachetteGo.com
Facebook.com/HachetteGo
Instagram.com/HachetteGo

First Edition: December 2024

Published by Hachette Go, an imprint of Hachette Book Group, Inc. The Hachette Go name and logo are trademarks of the Hachette Book Group.

The Hachette Speakers Bureau provides a wide range of authors for speaking events. To find out more, visit hachettespeakersbureau.com or email HachetteSpeakers@hbgusa.com.

Hachette Go books may be purchased in bulk for business, educational, or promotional use. For information, please contact your local bookseller or email the Hachette Book Group Special Markets Department at Special.Markets@hbgusa.com.

The publisher is not responsible for websites (or their content) that are not owned by the publisher.

Print book interior design by Amy Quinn.

Library of Congress Cataloging-in-Publication Data

Name: Martin, William, 1944– author.
Title: The daily Tao: 365 meditations on the Tao te ching / William Martin.
Description: First edition. | New York: Hachette Go, 2024. | Series: Day by day
Identifiers: LCCN 2023052060 | ISBN 9780306834837 (trade paperback) | ISBN 9780306834851 (ebook)
Subjects: LCSH: Taoist meditations. | Religious life—Taoism.
Classification: LCC BL1942.8 .M38 2024 | DDC 299.5/1435—dc23/eng/20240325
LC record available at https://lccn.loc.gov/2023052060

ISBNs: 978-0-306-83483-7 (trade paperback), 978-0-306-83485-1 (ebook)

Printed in the United States of America

LSC-C

Printing 1, 2024

For Nancy, as always.

Contents

Introduction

Welcome to the journey. This book is my invitation to you to join me in walking day by day along the path of the *Tao Te Ching* (*Dao De Ching*). This classic of Chinese wisdom poetry, written almost 2,600 years ago, is one of the most loved and widely translated books in human history. Its author is traditionally considered to be Lao-tzu, a Chinese sage who lived during the fifth century BCE. Scholars enjoy debating whether or not Lao-tzu actually authored the *Tao Te Ching.* Some contend that it is a compilation of the wisdom of several authors. I am not particularly concerned with this issue for the purposes of this book. Whoever the author or authors were, they have my everlasting gratitude.

For me, Lao-tzu's book has been much more than a beautiful collection of Chinese wisdom poetry. I have found it to be a *Tao*—which can be translated as "path"—that has opened for me the experience of life in all its beauty and all its pain. It has been a path for me into the territory of awareness, awakening, and living in the present moment. It has gently guided me to see how my conditioned mental habits restrict me, distract me, and cause me unnecessary suffering. Countless others, across the centuries, have found wisdom and guidance in this path. For this practice I offer Lao-tzu, whoever he was, my deepest thanks.

Walking the Tao

The only step necessary on this walk with the Tao is the one before you at this moment. In fact, this is the only step possible for you. All the other steps along the way are theoretical and will not be real until they, too, lie directly in your path. I am still walking along this same journey and I offer you the companionship of my words in the hopes that they may be of some guidance to you. The walk itself, however, is yours alone to walk.

As you proceed day by day, you will be encountering the *Tao Te Ching* in a piecemeal manner. Each line is taken from a chapter (noted in parentheses) and presented as a stand-alone thought. This can be confusing, and it might be helpful to have a translation of the *Tao Te Ching* available. The translation I am using in this volume (at the back of the book) is my own, taken from the book *A Path and a Practice*, published by Hachette Books. No matter the translation, the text of the *Tao Te Ching* is not a linear text. It does not set out its premises at the beginning and then build and expand on them in a logical progression. Each chapter is a small piece of poetry that looks at a slice of life from the perspective of Lao-tzu's philosophy. It can be frustrating for those of us who are conditioned to assume that, in order to be helpful, books must be orderly and linear.

Yet life is not orderly. We perceive that life unfolds in a linear fashion because our brain processes it one moment after another. But life itself is actually an infinitely complex dance in which we participate, but of which we catch only limited glimpses. It is filled with twists, turns, backtracks, rest stops, and steep grades. Just when we think we can't climb another step, the trail opens up to a restful meadow. Just as we are relaxing along a babbling brook, a canyon appears and the trail plunges into shadow and danger. It is an ever-changing path and each moment is new. Lao-tzu's book has these same characteristics. As you walk the daily walk, keep this in mind. Each day is new, but the basic themes repeat.

Direct Experience

Lao-tzu was neither a priest nor a follower of any religious belief system. He was a patient observer of the flow of life. He watched the wind move the clouds across the sky and the rain soak the earth. He watched rivers flow through wide valleys and tumble down mountain canyons. He watched the crane stand patiently by the lakeside, waiting on one leg until the water cleared to reveal a fish. He considered the contentment of the turtle sitting in the mud. He observed crops flourish one year and fail the next. He watched the seasons come and go. He saw the wonder of all things rising and falling, coming and going, living and dying. He came to understand that life cannot be captured by words and concepts. It can be talked about. It can be thought about. But it cannot be truly fathomed. It can only be experienced.

The legends that surround the formation of the *Tao Te Ching* illustrate Lao-tzu's reluctance to put his teachings into written words. One such legend speaks of a time when he became so fed up with the politics of repression in the China of his day that he got on his ox and left the country. But the border guard would not let him leave until he wrote down his wisdom for all to share. Lao-tzu said, "If I write it down, it will no longer be the Tao." Nevertheless, the guard would not let him leave until he wrote something. So he dismounted his ox, sat in the shade of a tree, and in one afternoon wrote the short text of poetic wisdom that resonates to the present day.

This legend illustrates that this path is not one of abstract philosophy. It is a way of looking at the processes of life as they actually are, not as we think they are. It is a path that must be walked moment by moment, not discussed in endless words. Yet using thoughts and words to make sense of our experience is what we humans do. It is part of our nature. Lao-tzu uses words in short poetic stanzas so they might serve as guides and gateways to direct experience rather than as mere abstractions and distractions. This sometimes frustrates our Western conditioning under which we have come to expect things to be fully explained without ambiguity or paradox.

Directly experiencing life is not something we do easily. By the time we are adults, our experience is mediated through filters that provide a constant commentary *about* our life but that ignore the thing itself. We come to believe that life is what we see on a screen. This process is so deeply conditioned in most of us that we don't even notice it. We wander day after day with our minds spinning an endless stream of thoughts, judgments, hopes, fantasies, critiques, and plans all mixed with a babel of advertising jingles and fragments of YouTube videos.

Lao-tzu suggests that this mediated experience is not the same as actual life. At the same time, he does not totally discount the conceptual thinking process. We make a certain kind of sense out of life through the use of categories, thoughts, and words. But these must be seen as gateways to life, not life itself.

Present Moment

Living in the present moment is an essential component of this path. There is no place to go except here. There is no one to be except who you are right now. This is difficult to grasp. As soon as we actually turn to the present moment, a thought arises that casts our attention toward some future event or to something in the past. It is almost as if the present moment is too frightening to actually experience. An internal voice suggests that we are in too much physical or emotional pain. It hints that we really don't have the capacity to directly face this moment. It then presents an alternative from the countless diversions and distractions available.

We may also notice a voice that tells us, "If you live in the present moment, you will stop all forward progress. You will just drift through life." This voice makes suggestions for self-improvement, indicating that, "Some later day you will have things arranged so the present moment will be acceptable. Until then, keep on striving!"

Other voices suggest that the present moment is impractical, naive, selfish, lazy, or impossible. They present the usual daydreams, fantasies, and mental babble to keep us distracted and unconscious. Thus, such a simple-sounding thing as "living in the present moment" can actually be quite a challenge. Lao-tzu noticed this same difficulty and gently offers other themes throughout his little book to support and encourage this practice of "the present moment."

Opposites

This walk does not eliminate the uncomfortable, the painful, or any of the things and qualities we have learned to call "negative." It would be more popular if it promised to eliminate these things. Instead, it promises that we will learn to see the polarities of life in an entirely different way. It affirms that polarity is essential to the fabric of existence. The mysterious world of quantum physics reveals this basic truth. The electron with its "negative" charge and the proton with its "positive" charge exist within the atom in perfect balance. Without this fundamental "yin and yang" of atomic structure, nothing would exist.

Our basic perception of existence is that of polarities: here and there, us and them, up and down, love and fear, joy and sorrow, life and death. We naturally prefer those things that seem "positive"; therefore, much of our life is spent trying to experience them in isolation from their "negative" complements. This impossible task only increases our fear and frustration. No matter how hard we try to make it otherwise, rising always gives way to falling, having always gives way to losing, and life always gives way to death.

Walking this path expands our vision and gives us a vantage point where we see all these polarities contained within a greater space. Life gives way to death, but death turns and makes way for life. We don't waste energy challenging the processes of life and instead work in cooperation with them. The negative becomes the doorway to the positive. The positive is fully enjoyed without clinging. We become capable of experiencing the whole of life rather than just the parts we prefer. Our life is not limited by our fears. Freedom becomes a permanent quality of life available anywhere, anytime.

Acceptance

Acceptance is courageous attention turned to the nature of things as they truly are, not as we wish them to be. This kind of attention enables our natural wisdom and energy to work effectively with the given circumstances. It allows us to avoid the twin traps of hiding our head in the sand while events roll over us and making things worse and wearing ourselves out by frenetic and ineffective activity. Acceptance allows us to fully understand events and circumstances so that we can participate in life with freedom and joy. We become as patient as a still pond yet powerful as a rushing river.

Our conditioning will insist that, if we accept life as it is, it will never change. We will become the passive victims of fate. In fact, Lao-tzu insists, just the opposite is true. Without a deep and courageous acceptance of the "is-ness" of life, our actions become distorted by our need to impose our opinions, ideas, and solutions on life without understanding the true nature of things. We then stand outside of situations and attempt to fix them from this vantage point. This approach has never worked and it never will. Nonacceptance keeps patterns intact. Acceptance sets us free.

Universal

Lao-tzu is distrustful of formal religion and does not talk about belief systems. He does not advocate the esoteric form of Taoist religion that was prevalent in the China of his time—a Taoism of magic, rituals, and beliefs. His path stands outside such practices and asks nothing from those who follow it except that they pay attention. It does not present rules and doctrines to which one must assent. It presents only observations of the way the Tao seems to work in everyday life and encourages us to follow the same pattern in our lives.

This path is available to persons of any religious tradition or of no tradition. It does not require that we give up rituals, nor does it require that we adopt any. Christians, Buddhists, Muslims, and atheists are all equally welcome. There are no "people of the Tao" who are set apart from any other people. Everything and everyone in the cosmos are expressions of the Tao. Everyone emerges from the Tao and everyone is contained within the Tao.

The only distinction Lao-tzu would make is the observation that those who practice mindful attention to the ways of the Tao will experience the contentment, freedom, and joy that come from understanding oneself to be a part of life in all its mystery and wonder. It is as if someone within us draws a huge, even infinite, circle that takes in everything that is and then says, "To this I belong!"

True Nature

In these pages I use phrases such as "conditioned thinking" and "conditioning" to refer to that part of our self-identity that arises from our need to find safety and belonging within our families, communities, societies, and world. Our brain naturally processes information in a discrete manner, separating an almost infinite array of sensory input into separate categories of "this" and "that." After a few years of this process, we develop a sense of ourselves as a "self," as one more "this" separate from all the other "thats." The concern for the survival and well-being of this conditioned self creates a life of fear, tension, resistance, and suffering.

There is nothing wrong with this process. It is part of life. The problem arises, says Lao-tzu, when we mistake this conditioned self for our true nature, when we believe that this is who we really are rather than just a limited way of seeing ourselves. This is a necessary stage of our development, but a stage that must be transcended in order to experience the full freedom life has to offer.

Lao-tzu uses the character *p'u*, which literally means "uncarved block," to indicate the part of our nature that is not conditioned. It is our original or true nature. It exists outside of our ego structures and stands apart from all our conditioned fears. Within our true nature, change, loss, pain, separation, and death all take their turns as our life unfolds but are not overlaid with a blanket of fear and resistance.

This is not a "self-improvement" path. Our true nature does not need improvement. Our conditioned mind gravitates toward self-improvement programs because they ensure that there will always be a "self" to improve. Paradoxically, as we discover our true nature, the peace and joy that self-improvement programs promise actually appear. This peace and joy, however, is no longer dependent on the fragile foundation of self-effort. Peace and joy arise because they are integral to our true nature. We are not making ourselves into some sort of spiritual ideal. We are discovering who and what we already truly are.

Letting Go

Because we feel we are somehow separate from life, we conclude that our safety and well-being are dependent on our ability to control our circumstances. When we try to control circumstances, we separate ourselves from those circumstances to such a degree that we end up bringing ourselves and others misery instead of the promised safety. Lao-tzu teaches us to let go. We let go of the belief that control is possible. We let go of the notion that control will keep us safe. We let go of the countless conditioned beliefs that promise safety and happiness but end up causing anxiety and suffering. We eventually let go of the ideas of who we are as separate egos.

Growing an ego is part of the human condition. But this path suggests that this development might be just one stage of human development rather than its end product. Developing a cocoon is a natural and essential part of being a caterpillar. But the time comes when the cocoon softens, wears out, and opens up. What if this is the case for all the opinions, possessions, and ego identities that we think are so necessary? What if, when the cocoon of ego softens, instead of the feared abyss we find a butterfly?

Flexibility

Lao-tzu often uses water as a symbol for the power of flexibility. All water on earth has its origins in the ocean. From the ocean it rises to the clouds, drifts across the sky, and begins its return to the ocean. Sometimes it falls directly onto the ocean. Sometimes it falls on land and makes its way back to the ocean through streams, lakes, and rivers. Whatever water meets along the way, it embraces. Yet nothing stops it from returning. It does not ask if it is taking the "right" path to its home. It knows that all paths are paths of return. It is patient, powerful, and irresistible. Obstacles are never a problem. It will flow around, cascade over, seep under, wear away, or evaporate and fall on the other side of any obstacle.

Our conditioning will characterize flexibility as wishy-washy, indecisive, weak, and ineffective. Our mental habits insist that the best way of meeting obstacles is to resist, fight, defeat, and destroy whatever blocks us from our goals. On this path, however, we do not need to fight and destroy. We will overcome any seeming obstacle in the same manner water overcomes—patience and flexibility. The ultimate success of our journey is assured; therefore, we relax and allow ourselves to fully embrace and understand our current situation that seems to be an obstacle. As we understand, we flow naturally to the next appropriate step. Our rigidity dissolves and we smoothly accomplish whatever is necessary.

Effortless

Lao-tzu makes extensive use of the character combination *wu wei*, which literally means "not doing." This phrase implies pure action in the present moment without any accompanying resistance, second-guessing, or worry. We just "do what we do." The more awareness we bring to the present moment, the more wu wei is possible. Wu wei can take the form of relaxed and patient waiting or energetic action.

Wu wei is not passive, though it may sometimes seem that way when its wisdom indicates relaxed stillness in the midst of the frantic conditioned messages that say, "Hurry, hurry, hurry, do something!" Wu wei waits in stillness until the time is right. Then, energetic action flows like a rushing river and we accomplish the task with energy but without strain.

With wu wei, we are not being constantly drawn off into past memories or future fantasies. We are focused on the moment and we know intuitively just what to do without second-guessing. We become expansive and creative. We take into account a multitude of factors without being overloaded. Thoughts arise and pass away without distracting us from the task of the moment. Life flows.

Stillness

Taoist stillness is a simple practice. It requires no special equipment, atmosphere, or preparation. It can be helpful to have a comfortable chair or cushion, but it is not necessary. Many people enjoy standing stillness. Stillness is the simple cultivation of the ability to be in a restful but alert state of consciousness wherever we are.

Stillness is not a way of creating altered states of consciousness. In fact, most of modern life is spent in altered states of consciousness created by the cacophony of media. Stillness is the practice of returning to an unaltered state. We simply sit or stand quietly and pay attention to the way the breath enters and leaves the body. We allow our thoughts to go wherever they will and we gently return our attention to our breath and cease to follow the thoughts.

We are not trying to change anything. We are simply watching and understanding how our mind works and how it sees and interprets events. We gradually understand how we have been conditioned to resist, distract, divert, worry, plan, and in general avoid actually living our lives. As we see this process, we learn to return again and again to the present moment by simply noticing our breath.

Stillness may be uncomfortable at first. Our mind has been creating turmoil for decades and stopping to pay attention to it is, at first, not much fun. But eventually stillness becomes a primary strategy for keeping our attention peaceful and centered in the moment. We learn to be still because, in stillness, we find that we actually wake up to our lives.

The Next Step

No matter how vast the chasm between where we feel we are and where we sense we are going, the only action we can ever take is the one simple step that lies in front of us right in this moment. No matter how complex the journey seems, we only need to know to take the next small step, then the next one, then the next.

Let's Begin

Our way of walking this path together will be to consider one or two lines of Lao-tzu's poetry each day. We will let these lines resonate in our minds for the entire day and see what effect they might have on our life. I have used lines from my own translation of the *Tao Te Ching* for this practice, but you might want to have other translations available to aid you in going deeper. My own translation is written from a modern perspective of using the poetry as a guide for daily life.

For each day's verse I have added some thoughts that might help clarify the theme. Or they might not. In that case, ignore them. Themes repeat and we will encounter the same aspects of the path from many vantage points. The journey is yours and your understanding will arise from deep within your own nature. I have also added suggestions for brief "breath prayers," a few words that might help your mind quiet down and absorb the themes. Again, modify them any way you wish to make the daily practice most helpful for you.

As you walk along, remember that you are not alone. This path has been walked by countless others throughout history and is being walked by countless fellow pilgrims at the present moment. Everyone seeking a way of awakening, truth, and present-moment living is your companion on this path, whatever religious or non-religious label they might currently wear. They have come from all lands, carrying with them a diversity of cultural and religious expressions. They have called themselves Taoists, Buddhists, Christians, Jews, Sufis, Muslims, atheists, and countless other names. They have established this path with compassion and mindfulness. All their sorrows and all their joys have become part of the landscape along this path. As you walk along, one step at a time, you will be walking in their footsteps. The only quality you need is a tiny bit of willingness. The only action you need to take is to lift your foot and take the next step.

THE DAILY TAO

Daily Practice

1

Talking about a path is not walking that path. (1)

Conventional wisdom insists that we make meaning out of life by our words and concepts, that our linguistic ability is what separates us from other animals. Yet every time we utter a word, we put a bit of distance between ourselves and life itself. The more words we use, the greater the distance becomes until we are so separate and alone that we live in constant fear and misery. There is a place for words, but we must use them carefully.

- Take some time today completely free from words—spoken, written, heard, viewed, texted, or tweeted. How does it feel?

Talking . . . is not walking my path.

2

Thinking about life is not living. (1)

Our conscious thinking process has become a jumble of words. We have been taught to name things, define things, dissect things, atomize things, and explain things—all in an attempt to gain some illusion of control over the Mystery of Life. This again separates us from the very life for which we search with our words and thoughts. That which we seek will be found when the thinking words cease.

- Take ten minutes and look around. Notice how your thoughts are conditioned to name things. Can you just let things be without names?

Thinking is not . . . living.

3

Directly experiencing life brings unconditional appreciation and unity. (1)

A "friend" on Facebook is not a true friend. It is an image of a friend. Social media is not truly society. It is an imitation of society, and the longer it serves as a substitute for the real thing, the more lonely we become. A video of a mountain stream is not a substitute for sitting on a rock beside the real thing. When we cease trying to control life by images and concepts, we begin to see life as it actually is in each moment.

- Note the ways you keep yourself at a distance from the simple present moment. Again, let the words fade and notice the moment—without words, without thoughts. How does that feel?

I am not . . . my image.

4

Thinking about life brings conditional judgments and separation. (1)

Our word-filled thoughts enable us to pass judgment on each moment. Each judgment of the moment, whether we consider it "good" or "bad," separates us from life. We have been taught that we must judge things in order to survive, but this judging process has a dark side. It diminishes our natural joy and celebration of the roller-coaster ride of life.

- If you are not your thoughts, perhaps you are someone who thinks. Can you imagine yourself separate from your thoughts?

I am not . . . my thoughts.

5

Free of conditioned thinking, we experience our true nature. Caught in conditioned thinking, we experience only who we think we are. (1)

Conditioned thinking might be called "second thoughts." Conditioned thinking is seldom able to savor the present moment. Our "first thoughts" process direct experience. Second thoughts, however, attach labels, evaluations, and meanings. To an extent, these second thoughts are natural, but we must take care to understand the difference between the two ways of thinking.

- Look around you. What are your first thoughts? What are your second thoughts?

I want to know . . . my first thoughts.

6

Yet both our conditioned nature and our true nature are part of life itself. Our conditioned experience of living is a gateway to unconditional life. (1)

For all the dangers of our words and concepts, if we approach them carefully, they can be a gateway to the reality they attempt to represent. Understanding this requires that we take a step back from our conditioned ways of viewing thoughts and words. We awaken to the idea that, though we have thoughts, we are not those thoughts; though we use words, these words are not the "thing itself."

- Are there words in your experience that you recognize as gateways to something more Mysterious?

My words . . . are gateways.

7

Beauty cannot exist without ugliness. Virtue cannot exist without vice. (2)

The concepts we think of as "opposites" are, in reality, like the poles of a magnet. A magnet, by its very nature, must have a north and a south pole or it would not have a magnetic field. The cosmos is, in its very nature, composed of a quantum atomic structure that has inseparable positive and negative poles that dance in constant motion. When we try to pretend that we can have only beauty, only light, only progress, only gain, or only anything, we open ourselves to suffering.

- Think of the opposites in your life. Now think of these as inseparable parts of a whole. Allow them to coexist. How does that feel?

I am a part . . . of it all.

8

Living, we know death. Struggling, we know ease. Rising high, we know the depths. Being quiet, we understand noise. (2)

For the physical universe to exist, the proton and the electron, positive and negative, must exist. For physical life to exist, there must be death to limit and balance it. Gain must be balanced by loss or it would destroy us. Sound must imply silence or music would not exist. It all belongs together.

- Imagine living forever in your current body and form. Sounds great? Really? Imagine succeeding without effort, always. Great? Really? How does the interplay of negativity and positivity shape your life?

I accept . . . it all.

9

Everything gives rise to its opposite; therefore, we work without conscious effort and teach without agenda. (2)

This verse introduces the Taoist concept of wu wei, "action without resistance." The harder we try to make things work, the more we activate the fear that we will not succeed. The more we fear failure, the more desperate our actions become and the less effective our work will be. Wu wei does not mean idleness. It means acting without trying to force things.

- Can you remember a time when your actions seemed effortless? Are you trying too hard right now?

I act . . . with ease.

10

We enjoy everything and possess nothing. (2)

The idea that we must possess, own, control, and accumulate in order to enjoy life is nonsense. The moment our thoughts constrict around a thing or an idea, the joy for which we hoped is lost. This truth is at the heart of every authentic spiritual tradition. The only way to enjoy anything, any experience, any love, or any accomplishment is to let it flow in and out of our life, never grasping, always enjoying.

- Are you grasping anything right now? An idea? A possession? A love? Imagine your life as a flowing river, always carrying things away and always bringing more.

I let it go . . . let it flow.

11

Our accomplishments do not emerge from our ego, so we do not cling to them. Thus they benefit all beings. (2)

There is a great danger in taking life personally. Egocentrism is really a miserable way to live. Ego is merely a constellation of personas, or masks, that we have created to present a face to the external world. We come to believe that it is who we are, but it is only a mask. When we take this mask to be the truth, we suffer because we are always evaluating, comparing, and refining something that is not real, not our authentic being.

- Are you taking yourself (that is, images of who you think you are) too seriously? What if this image is not all that important?

I am not . . . my ego.

12

If achievement is valued, jealousy will result. If possessions are valued, hoarding and stealing will result. (3)

Everyone values achievement. Wanting possessions is normal. Right? This verse does seem contrary to conventional wisdom, but then the *Tao Te Ching* is exactly that—contrary to conventional wisdom. Achieving and possessing things are so often attempts to feel secure. It never works. We will always feel at risk of failing and losing no matter how frantically we work and try to protect ourselves.

- What feelings of envy do you experience? Do you hoard things? Does it satisfy you?

I let . . . things go.

13

Therefore, this path is one of contentment and simplicity. (3)

Contentment cannot exist without simplicity, but it's not necessarily that easy. Authentic simplicity is actually a complicated and evolving perception of what we truly need to be happy. The important thing is not to let an avaricious society define the parameters of contentment. Society does not value contentment. It needs discontentment to keep the economy chugging along.

- What do you need to be content? Truly? What if I waved my magic Taoist wand and made you absolutely content, just as you are now? How would your life change?

I am simple . . . and content.

14

It empties our mind of its chattering and fills our soul with truth. (3)

Our minds are filled with chatter, boring, endless chatter. Buddhists call it "monkey mind." It's actually more like "adolescent monkey who broke into their parent's liquor cabinet mind." The Tao path is one of a quiet mind. The monkey chatter stops. Mindfulness, meditation, qigong, yoga, and many other practices can guide us in this quieting, but whatever the methods, we must cultivate a still mind.

- Start with small steps. Take fifteen seconds and let your vision soften and your thoughts fade. You are not your thoughts. What, then, are you?

I let my thoughts fade . . . and discover myself.

15

It frees us from our wanting and returns us to our passion. (3)

Wanting something and being passionate about something are entirely different energies. Despite what romance novels tell us, "I want you" is not a declaration of love or passion. It is narcissistic claptrap. Passionate love affairs are often simply wanting on steroids. Authentic passion is the fulfillment of the purpose for which our souls were designed. Authentic passion comes from the flow of the Tao within us.

- What do you want? What are you passionate about? Can you sense the difference?

I want . . . my passion.

16

No longer needing to have our own way, we are not fooled by clever plots and plans. (3)

Plots and plans are the engines of the economy. Billions of dollars are invested in algorithms, research, and platforms like YouTube, Instagram, and Google in order to come up with clever plots and plans. These are *tremendously* clever. We will be fooled unless we stop engaging them. *Planning is greatly overrated.* I know, it seems crazy to say, but after a year with the Tao you will have an entirely new view of planning.

- How much time do you spend plotting and planning to get what you want? If you stopped plotting and planning, what would happen? Really?

I let my plots and plans . . . slip into a quiet mind.

17

Our actions become focused, pure, and effortless. (3)

This path is an entirely new way of acting in the world. As we said earlier, this energy is called wu wei. It means "action without resistance." It is action that is done not by our conditioned ego mind but by the movement of the Tao itself. In the title of the book *Tao Te Ching*, *Te* means "natural virtue or power that flows from the Tao." *Ching* means "book." So, we have "*The Book of the Way of Natural Power.*"

- Think of a time when you were focused, not because you tried but because it just happened. You can't make this happen, but you can let it happen if you practice.

My actions . . . are without resistance.

18

Walking this path, we experience inexhaustible energy. (4)

It is not that we don't become tired. It is that our tiredness has a different quality from the exhausted, wrung-out, and depleted feeling that our tension-filled actions usually produce. We're not trying as hard to push the river. We learn when to move quickly and when to slow down, when to act and when to rest—unaffected by the external pushes and pulls that used to dominate us.

- Make a note of tired feelings. Can you distinguish different types of tiredness? How are they different? What makes the difference?

I work . . . and don't grow weary.

19

From what appears an empty void, we find the bounty of life. (4)

Don't be afraid of emptiness. The empty quantum flux of the universe gave birth to infinite forms and wonders. Our culture wants to fill every moment with noise, but it is the still, quiet, and empty moment that births creativity. New ideas, new approaches, and new ways of living come to us when we stop believing the noise that drives us in the endless circles of the rat race.

- Don't be afraid of the quiet and still moments. See them as gifts. Cultivate them. Set aside five minutes today to create a time for emptiness.

I come . . . to the quiet.

20

Our edginess, tension, anger, and turmoil begin to settle down . . . (4)

Life is not meant to be lived "on edge." Much social media is designed to keep us "edgy," as if that is a good thing. It is not. Our souls long for something deeper, something more authentic. Authentic living emerges when the artificial edginess fades away. We find that we can be "energized" without the tense, anxiety-driven feeling.

- Take a media fast for a day.

I can lose . . . my edge.

21

. . . and we find a deep tranquility that has been here waiting since before the beginning of beginning-less time. (4)

Modern life has been chaotic for so long that we believe it could be no other way. In fact, we aren't sure we want it to be otherwise. Tranquility makes us nervous, as if another shoe is about to drop. The Tao, however, for all its flow and change, moves from a place of deep peace. That place is waiting for us at every moment, no matter how busy and pressured that moment might seem. It is our natural state of being.

- In what ways do you avoid tranquility? Why?

I am willing . . . to be tranquil.

22

Life has no preferences. Every manifestation has its place and lives its life under the sun. (5)

Life may not have preferences, but we sure have them. We prefer health to sickness, joy to sorrow, success to failure, and security to chaos. The Tao, however, seems not to take our wishes into account. Instead it asks us to align ourselves with its flow rather than the other way around. Strangely, when we let it have its way (as if we have a choice), something shifts inside us that loosens our tension. Options we never considered pop into being.

- You don't have to pretend you don't have them, but what preferences might you hold with a looser grip?

I hold my preferences . . . lightly.

23

Therefore, we welcome everything and everyone without distinction. (5)

Welcoming everything and everyone does not mean we approve of or like everything and everyone. Remember that we are experimenting with a path and a practice that runs counter to everything we "know" to be true. So our practice is not just to cultivate an attitude of acceptance but also to go for the real prize and *welcome* everything and everyone that arise. Because what is . . . is, why not welcome it?

- Pick a situation you are currently facing and say aloud, "This is part of my life and my life is part of the Tao, so I welcome this!" (It is sort of like saying, "Bring it on!")

I welcome life . . . bring it on.

24

Life continuously breathes its forms into existence, never depleting itself, always replenishing itself. (5)

We don't exhaust the air we breathe because the earth transforms our exhalation into new energy. In this way the Tao breathes in and out, creating forms and returning those forms to the source from where they will once again be breathed into new forms. If we relax and trust this process, we will find renewal waiting for us in each breath.

- Don't take your breath for granted. Pay attention to this fundamental wonder and protect it.

I breathe in new . . . I breathe out old.

25

Clinging to our preferences, we separate ourselves from life and suffer exhaustion. (5)

The question of preferences arises once again. Having preferences is natural. Clinging to them causes suffering and exhaustion. Preferring a particular outcome and working toward it is also natural. Clinging to that outcome separates us from the possibilities offered to us in the midst of any situation. Are you willing to allow new possibilities?

- Make a list of five things you truly prefer. It could be as simple as broccoli over chard or as complex as a new way of living. Ask whether these preferences shut out unexpected possibilities.

I am open . . . to the possibilities.

26

Sitting still and following our breath, we find renewal. (5)

There is a place within us, just below our navel, midway to our spine. It is our center, the place where our energy gathers itself. It is the still point from which all movement begins. When we are off-balance and filled with restless energy, we can return our attention to this point. Being "centered" is only partly a metaphor. There is a physical place at which our balance and tranquility dwell. It is important to know this place.

- Sit still for five minutes with your hands resting gently over your navel. Let your abdomen expand as you breathe in and contract as you breathe out. This is the center.

I come . . . to the still point.

27

Everything that exists was born of the feminine principle within the Tao. This mysterious principle can be called "the mother of all." (6)

The Tao sees this feminine principle as the source of all existence. Sometimes religions see the cosmos as the creation of a Father God, made and built and formed by masculine energy. The Tao sees it from a different perspective. The cosmos was not made by some external craftsman. It was born from deep inside the Tao. Being born is quite different from being made. We are born of the Tao and therefore never separate from that Tao.

- What difference does it make to you to think of "being born" instead of "being made"? Which is more intimate, more connective?

I am born . . . of the Tao.

28

There is no need to weary ourselves in an effort to find her. She is ever with us because she "is" us. (6)

The Tao does not stand apart from us, waiting for us to pray the right words or believe the right formula. The Tao is living "as" us in each moment. It is our conditioned mind that "thinks" that we are separate and alone. Our deeper Tao mind is not, never has been, and never will be separate and alone. We experience both minds. The question is, which mind will we believe and trust?

- Pretend for a moment that you believe that you are "being lived" by the Tao. What would be different about your day?

I am lived . . . by the Tao.

29

How can we find the eternal, the lasting nature of the Tao that seems so elusive amid the changes of life? The Tao does not come and go, as do all formations. The Tao is the watcher of the comings and the goings. (7)

Life seems a mystery to us. It is filled with joys and sorrows, never stable and fixed. We wonder where we can put our trust. Life seems to end in death, which is impossible for our minds to grasp. Are we truly just a brief candle flame flickering in the wind, destined to be snuffed as if we never existed? It is difficult, but we can't avoid it. We must face life armed only with the question, who and what am I, really?

- Imagine that you are not the one who comes and goes, but the one who watches. Imagine "watching" your life from a place of eternal safety. How does it feel?

I am . . . the one who watches.

30

In our practice we find that we are the watchers as well. We watch our opinions and ideas, but we do not identify with them. (7)

Having opinions is quite different from identifying with those opinions. Our political landscape suffers immensely from *identification.* We don't merely hold certain political ideas, we *are these things.* Thus, dialogue is impossible. It would be far too threatening, so politics becomes a mere shouting match. We do not simply have "Republican" or "Democratic" opinions. We *are* Republicans or Democrats.

- Who are you independent of political opinions? Can you simply watch your opinions?

I am not . . . my opinions.

31

We watch our likes and dislikes but do not identify with them. (7)

Liking and disliking are natural parts of our conditioned mind. "Liking" something is often learned from what those around us seem to approve of. Sometimes we have an intrinsic liking of a taste or other sensation. We like some people and not others, often because of subconscious conditioning and societal norms. It is a complex process. The important practice is to remain somewhat distant from the likes and dislikes by remembering we are the awareness behind the liking.

- Think of a food that you like. What about this food makes it "likable"? Try the same process with a food you don't like. What makes it "unlikable"? Just notice these thoughts.

Like . . . not like . . . same thing.

32

We watch our desires and our fears but do not identify with them. (7)

Desire feels more potent than simply liking something. Desire can be overwhelming and obsessive and is usually coupled with fear. The more we desire something, the more we fear losing it. To fear something is to desire its opposite. Not identifying with fears and desires is more difficult than not identifying with mere preferences. Still, it remains an essential part of practice. We can feel desire and fear but not be lost in them.

- What do you fear most? Notice that this feeling of fear is real, but it is not the definition of who you truly are. You feel a fear, but you are not this fear.

I am neither . . . my fears . . . nor my desires.

33

When these things arise, we watch. When they pass away, we remain. (7)

All our mental formations such as ideas, opinions, likes, dislikes, fears, desires, and worries are simply that—mental formations. They all pass away. Our bodies also pass away. Somehow we remain. Taoism does not have a particular belief about life after death, only the awareness that the being/energy/soul who is experiencing life as "us" remains.

- Everything passes away, but you remain. This is impossible to understand with a limited conditioned mind, but if you practice stillness and calmness, you will sense its truth.

I . . . remain.

34

Our true nature is like water. It doesn't decide that some tasks are too distasteful. It just flows like a river to the ocean, nurturing everything in its path. (8)

Taoist thought is often called "The Watercourse Way." Lao-tzu says that we, in our true nature, are like water and naturally nurture whatever is in our path. If we lay aside all the conditioned judgments and opinions that get in the way, we are naturally kind to whatever comes our way. It doesn't mean that we have to pretend that we like something that we don't like. It simply means that we can always act with kindness, even if that kindness consists of remaining silent.

- Imagine a situation that makes you feel uncomfortable and judgmental. Is there a natural kindness within you that you can call upon? You don't have to pretend. You just have to relax and see if something within you knows what to say or do.

My nature . . . is kindness.

35

This is the nature of the Tao within all people. (8)

This path is not just about us. It is about every living being. We are not a special case of awareness and compassion. The Tao is the true nature of all life. It is important that we learn to see the world through eyes that recognize this truth. Everything within our experience today is filled with the essence of the Tao and is therefore of the same essence as are we.

- Nothing you see is separate from you. Nothing you see is different, at the core, from you. How does this feel?

All I see . . . is part of me.

36

Living by this principle, we choose dwellings that are simple and humble. (8)

In 1950, the median size of a single-family home in the United States was 1,500 square feet. By 2007, the size of a single-family home had increased to 2,500 square feet. In that same time period, the number of people per household actually decreased. It's natural to seek a comfortable dwelling, but have we allowed our conditioned mind to lead us into unnecessary debt and worry? Should a home be an investment? Really?

- What is the purpose of a house? What do you really need? Does the rising housing market make it unaffordable for some? What does it mean to live simply?

My needs . . . are simple.

37

We meditate to cultivate quiet and serene thoughts. (8)

Meditation is a broad term. The cultivation of a quiet, serene mind can take many forms, but some practice of quieting and stillness is necessary. It is important not to make meditation into one more thing that we have to do right. Qigong, the gentle meditative movement that includes taiji, is an effective practice. A quiet mind is a basic human birthright and is a necessary element of a well-lived life.

- If you don't have a meditative practice, experiment and find one that works for you. Don't make it a task, but instead find a form that is pleasant and effective—whatever contributes to serenity.

I am quiet . . . and serene.

38

We treat all beings with loving-kindness. (8)

Loving-kindness begins with the way we treat ourselves. Kindness to ourselves is not ego indulgence or laziness. It is, instead, the fundamental mindset we have toward ourselves as a human being who is an inseparable part of the Tao. If we are not kind to ourselves, we fool ourselves thinking we can be kind to others. Only by first loving ourselves can we learn to expand this understanding to include all beings.

- How do you feel about yourself, really? You make mistakes, but are you essentially good and worthy of kindness? This is an important question that is deserving of deep reflection.

Kindness . . . is my nature.

39

We speak with compassion and clarity. (8)

Words are cheap and most of the words we hear in our society are useless, even harmful, noise. Let's not add to this cacophony. Let's speak less and listen more. Let's let our words be kind and without a hint of manipulation or dishonesty. As we practice this, we notice that we speak less often. Speaking less, we hear and see things that previously escaped our attention.

- Why do you speak? To persuade? To convince? To get your way? To be liked?

Being quiet . . . I see.

40

We manage our lives for the benefit of all beings. (8)

We live in a culture that insists that we accumulate and achieve. But why? We are the manager of this complex enterprise called "my life," and we must determine its purpose. How are the resources of this enterprise allocated? How will this enterprise evolve over the coming years? What makes it a successful enterprise? What does it create that is of value?

- You truly are the manager of a unique enterprise. Have you ever asked yourself what the purpose of it is? The Tao suggests that it is to be of benefit. How?

How . . . may I serve?

41

We live in awareness of the present moment and take action only when the time is right. (8)

The present moment is not just a nice concept that allows us to savor life as it passes by. It is an awareness that is necessary for effective action to be taken. Athletes are often skilled at the ability to slow down the perception of time so that they can shoot the basket, throw the pass, or swing the bat. The conditioned mind will usually act too hastily or too slowly. The Tao mind will act at the proper moment with the proper force.

- How do you know when the "time is right"? Is it an emotional, physical, or spiritual knowing?

When the time is right . . . I act.

42

In this manner our life flows like water and fulfills itself naturally. (8)

The invention of the clock has been a double-edged sword. Life is actually a constant flow rather than a series of discrete time intervals. Clock time, however, has increased our illusion of control over events. We think we have fenced in the moments of our lives like we fence in our yards and fields. We believe that this gives us control over life and over time itself. That is an illusion. A schedule is of limited benefit at best.

- Try minimizing your use of clocks, digital or otherwise. Use them only when necessary for appointments; otherwise, forget them and see how you perceive the flow of your life.

Flow . . . not force.

43

This is a path of letting go so there will be room to live. (9)

Our homes and offices are cluttered, but nothing like the chaos that characterizes our conditioned minds. Besides chattering like a drunken monkey, the conditioned mind holds a ton of useless information, fears, and hopes. Ninety percent of the thoughts we have today, we had yesterday. It would be good for us to toss out the crap and gradually get the sense of a spacious mind.

- Write down a persistent useless thought, something that feels like it has been on your mind forever. Wad up the paper. Throw it in the trash. Repeat for another thought.

Clean . . . my mind.

44

If we hold on to opinions, our minds will become dull and useless. Let go of opinions. (9)

Our opinions are simply perceptions, and all perceptions are, by nature, incomplete and not reflective of the whole reality of an object or event. One of the primary ways we grasp and retain our opinions is by sharing them. Is that really necessary? Almost every overheard conversation is some version of opinion-sharing. Who benefits from this barrage of limited perceptions?

- Can you keep your opinions to yourself? Practice it. It will eventually make your thinking sharper and more useful.

Opinions . . . float away.

45

If we hold on to possessions, we will always be at risk. Let go of possessions. (9)

Marie Kondo earns her living helping people toss stuff out. So do many other professional organizers. Yet we keep on accumulating stuff. Jesus told a parable about the futility of "bigger barns." In Taoist thought, the most fortunate person is the one who can leave home to escape a fire without having to think twice about saving anything.

- What five things would you grab if you had thirty seconds to leave a burning house? What does this say about the money and effort you spend getting and keeping objects and trinkets?

Owning nothing . . . I am free.

46

If we hold on to ego, we will continue to suffer. Let go of ego. (9)

We use the word *ego* to represent the constellation of personas, or identities, that the conditioned mind forms as we develop. These personas are the masks we present to the world in an attempt to define who we are and what our place in the world might be. Ego development is not wrong, but it leads us to suffer when we forget that these masks are not, in fact, our identity. We end up having to keep the masks in place, pretending even to ourselves.

- Think of the masks or roles you play every day. Are they really necessary? Can you drop them for just a few moments when you are with someone you love and trust? Can you drop them when you are alone and stop pretending to yourself?

I am not . . . the roles I play.

47

Working without thought of praise or blame is the way to true contentment. (9)

Isn't praise a good thing? Isn't it pleasant to receive compliments for a job well done? Of course praise is pleasant. But praise is just the flip side of blame. When our lives are spent seeking praise, we are afraid of and avoiding blame. Either way, the work itself suffers. Simply paying full and complete attention to what we are doing at the moment is sufficient.

- Whether you are washing dishes, entering data, or designing a building, don't think about praise or blame. Just think about the work itself.

Without praise . . . without blame.

48

Can we embrace both the acceptable and unacceptable parts of ourselves? (10)

The concepts of acceptable and unacceptable are, for the most part, illusions. The conditioning we receive from parents, teachers, and other authority figures teaches us to evaluate every aspect of our being according to certain standards. We separate ourselves into the two categories and try to enhance the acceptable and ignore or kill off the unacceptable. This divides us against ourselves and makes it difficult to develop compassion and forgiveness.

- Think of an "unacceptable" trait you wish was absent from your life. You don't have to condone or indulge this trait, but can you simply hold this part of yourself tenderly until it loosens and fades?

I accept myself . . . completely.

49

Can we breathe as easily as innocent babies? (10)

Innocence is a fundamental component of our true nature. Contrary to some religious doctrines, we are all born in innocence and in unity with the Tao. Only as our conditioned mind develops do we feel the separation and fear that constricts our muscles and makes our breathing labored and shallow. We can begin to reverse this process by starting with the act of breathing. Slow, relaxed breathing can help connect us to our true and essential nature.

- Count the number of breaths you take in a thirty-second period. Then see if you can lessen this number in the next thirty seconds. Don't breathe in an artificial manner. Just breathe a little deeper and a little slower.

Breathe in . . . breathe out.

50

Can we see the world clearly and without judgment? (10)

Our culture and society are deeply distorted and unhealthy. We can't pretend to see it otherwise. However, we can refrain from a sour and obsessive cynicism that, in turn, skews our ability to see clearly. We can simply accept that our culture is what it is and do our best to live as authentically, compassionately, and creatively as possible within the constraints it imposes.

- Do your opinions and judgments cause you to be constantly complaining to others and to yourself? Can you see how this can create a vicious circle that skews your ability to see clearly?

What is . . . is.

51

Can we act with loving-kindness, yet remain unknown and unsung? (10)

Do we really want to live our whole life unknown and unsung, anonymous, and under the radar? Most of us depend on recognition of some sort, don't we? Whether it's on social media or as employee of the month. It is hard to value anonymity in a culture that values only fame. How we act when absolutely no one could possibly know is what reveals who we truly are.

- What would your true self do when no one sees?

Who is the one . . . whom no one knows or sees?

52

Can we watch all things come and go, yet remain undisturbed? (10)

I am an elderly person. My body, though healthy, is showing its transient nature in countless little ways. I used to take every day for granted as a time of health and comfort. Now I am watching the whole experience of life come and go with remarkable speed. It is passing at the same rate for you. Somehow we must find a space within where this does not frighten us.

- Can you imagine a state of mind where you can watch this whole process of transience and still have complete peace? Cultivate that.

Life comes and goes . . . I remain.

53

Can we accept our countless thoughts and opinions, yet not take them seriously? If we can do this, we are acting according to the virtue that is naturally ours . . . (10)

We believe that it is only our thoughts that make our life. But is there a quality within us that stands apart from all these thoughts? If there is, then this is the quality that should guide our life. It should be the bottom line of our being. The *Tao Te Ching* calls this quality *Te*—or "natural virtue or power." Once again, we are reminded that we are not our thoughts.

- Assume that you are not simply the content of your mind, that there is something about you that is more than this. How might your life change if this is true?

I don't believe . . . my thoughts.

54

. . . nourishing all things but possessing nothing . . . (10)

Again we are forced to look at our ideas of possessing and owning things. Contrary to cultural norms, the Tao does not value private ownership, either by the individual or by the state. It sees capitalism and communism as equally misguided. Each system tends to worry more about control than about nourishment. Each system primarily values only the things we somehow control.

- It is a question of perspective. If you really don't own anything, then can you see everything as equally important and worthy of care?

Everything . . . is in my care.

55

. . . enjoying all things but clinging to nothing . . . (10)

Even in our skewed culture, life is filled with experiences and things that bring us joy without the need to control or possess them. A desert morning's sunrise is beautiful and absolutely free. We can go for a two-mile walk in the desert and feel the joy of our breath empowering our muscles. When sunrise is over, and the walk complete, there is no need to cling.

- What do you enjoy? Do you cling to it?

Enjoy it all . . . cling to nothing.

56

. . . working diligently but claiming credit for nothing . . . (10)

Why work without credit? Because it is actually the most enjoyable way to work. We are sold the idea that getting credit for our work is a necessary psychological reality. That is not really true. Work is a present-moment activity that is best savored for itself alone. All the conditioned thoughts about it are superfluous and actually diminish the joy. Do we really need to take credit for what we do?

- Stop looking for credit, just be present. Credit will take care of itself.

I work . . . because I enjoy it.

57

. . . growing in wisdom but controlling nothing. (10)

This idea of not controlling repeats itself again and again. That is because it is so difficult to integrate into modern life, which sees control as the be-all and end-all of contentment. Truly wise people, however, learn to adapt to the uncontrollability and unpredictability of life. They adapt to events and also to their own moods and to the moods of others.

- Relax today. Watch the waves of life and balance yourself as you get carried along.

No need . . . to control.

58

The spokes and the hub are the visible parts of the wheel. The wheel is useful because it spins about the invisible point at its center. (11)

Life today is chaotic and spinning, but there is a still point at the center of our own being. There are mornings when life seems a bit frightening and filled with demands we're not sure we can meet. Yet we can be aware, even if dimly, of that still point at our center from which we can observe events and thoughts. Remember to act from this point today.

- Rest your hands lightly over your abdomen. Take a deep breath. The point just below your navel is the center of your body. Use it as a reminder of the still point of your life.

I am . . . at my center.

59

Clay is the material from which a pot is made. The pot is useful because of the empty space inside the form. (11)

The essence, or mystery, of who we are is not to be found by examining our form, our body, or our brain. We are something "other" than the forms by which conditioning seeks to define us. It sounds strange to think of our true nature as "empty," but that is a way of saying that any description of ourselves is not us. We're something indefinable, empty.

- Being empty is liberation, isn't it? There is nothing you have to hold in place. Empty is not "nothing." It is "no particular thing"—perhaps you are Everything?

I am . . . empty.

60

A house is made with walls, doors, and windows. The house becomes a home for people through the quality of life lived within. (11)

In a culture obsessed with bigger and better and more, the quality of life has been lost. Houses, cars, gadgets, screens, phones, tablets, and the like have nothing to do with life. They are meaningless. Connection, compassion, and love are intangible yet are the only qualities worth pursuing. Cultivating these things is work enough for a lifetime.

- How much time do you spend on the essentials? Indeed, what are the essentials for you?

I am not . . . my things.

61

We practice with the visible and tangible, but it is the invisible and intangible within us that brings us life. (11)

All of chapter 11 in the *Tao Te Ching* points to the necessity of developing a strong inner life. Very little in our world values this, and we are seldom taught ways of cultivating our soul, our essence, our true nature. We go to jobs and buy our trinkets, watch our media, and go to bed, never asking, "What's it all about?"

- What is it all about? How will you find the answer to this question?

What is . . . it all about?

62

Trying to see everything, we become blind. (12)

Media today promises the clarity of information, but it is a misleading promise. Instead of clarity, we are blinded by an overwhelming barrage of images edited by people we don't know for purposes of their own. "Look here!" we are exhorted. "No. Look over there!" Our gaze is captured and we end up seeing nothing.

- Don't look at any media this evening. Can you do that? Many people in America cannot forgo the media for even one hour—a classic symptom of addiction.

Open . . . my eyes.

63

Listening to every voice, we become confused. (12)

Voices are everywhere. In the outer world and in our minds. Most of what we hear has its roots in fear of some sort. We are told to be afraid of being sick, being poor, or being different. We are badgered to believe half-truths offered by ignorant sources. Some of the insanity creeps past our defenses and we grow more and more uneasy.

- Stop listening! Turn it off. Walk away. Put on soothing music.

I turn . . . it all off.

64

Attempting to satisfy all our appetites, we become weary. (12)

Just about anywhere we turn, we are offered appetite stimulation—to buy more, consume more, do more. Complex algorithms track, understand, and predict our buying patterns and offer "suggestions" on almost every public website we frequent. We are like rats frantically pushing levers for some promised reward. Exhausting.

- When the rules of the game are stacked against you—don't play. What does it mean to disengage from a culture designed to enflame our appetites?

I'm not playing . . . anymore.

65

Being driven this way and that by our conditioning makes us crazy. (12)

Crazy for sure. Our conditioned minds are in charge and that is like the monkey managing the zoo. As long as the same minds remain in control, only superficialities will change. If we want transformational change, the first thing to change is our minds. That cannot be done by argument or polemic.

- There are no simple and quick methods for making this change. There is another "mind" within you. Where have you seen glimpses of it? How can you find it?

I am not . . . my conditioning.

66

Outer things exist, but do not define us. We are mysterious and internal, not obvious and external. (12)

The realization that we are, indeed, mysterious beings is the first step toward meaningful change. Knowing this, we cease settling for meaningless adjustments and futile attempts at fixing things. We develop a willingness to find the deeper, less traveled road. We become willing to actually transform ourselves.

- You are not who you think you are. Again, the way ahead is not clear and easy, but it is there for you when you are willing to enter the Mystery of yourself.

I am . . . a mystery.

67

Expecting either praise or blame makes us anxious. (13)

Anxiety arises whenever we are afraid of being found lacking. Only constant praise keeps this sense of "not enough" at bay, but who can keep that stream of praise flowing? Only by understanding that, no matter what, we *are* enough will we find rest. We will never understand that if we keep looking to culture for reassurance.

- If you truly are enough, then you can be healthy or sick, rich or poor, successful or unsuccessful. Stated simply, you can live until you die and be adequate for it all.

I am . . . adequate for my life.

68

Seeing ourselves as separate and isolated makes us suffer. (13)

The adequacy for which we long cannot be generated by our conditioned mind, which, by its very nature, sees itself as separate, alone, and vulnerable to all the vagaries of life. But if we see ourselves as an integral and inseparable part of life, then we belong. We are supported by every element of the cosmos wherever we are and whatever we experience. Separation is an illusion.

- Separation, however, is an extremely powerful and believable illusion. Everything culture asks of us depends on keeping this illusion in place. What keeps it in place for you? Can you drop that?

I always . . . belong.

69

Knowing that we are part of all that is, we care for and nurture all things as ourselves. (13)

Every spiritual tradition has some form of "love your neighbor as yourself" as central to its ethical code. When we understand our place as a part of Everything just like the cell is part of the body, this tradition takes on a deeper meaning. It is no longer an ethical nicety. It is a self-understanding that has the potential to transform the very nature of society.

- If other beings are no more separate from you than is your hand, how would your life change?

It's all . . . me.

70

What we are seeking can't be seen, heard, or touched. (14)

If we can't see it, hear it, or touch it, then what in the world are we doing? Yet there are ways of knowing that do not depend on these obvious sensory mechanisms. It may be easy to fool ourselves, but we have no choice but to look beyond the ordinary senses, which can only take us so far in our search.

- What do you know that you cannot see, hear, or touch?

I want to see . . . the unseen.

71

It is not obvious to the mind, but neither is it hidden from the heart. (14)

A Zen teacher once told me, "That which we are seeking is causing us to seek." This is another way of saying that seeking is unnecessary once we realize that "This is it!" Here. Now. Us. It's all One Thing Happening and, when the mind chatter quiets, we know it in our hearts.

- The heart, soul, or whatever you call it will show you the way. It will reveal itself without discursive thinking in every moment. Trust the self that exists beneath the thoughts.

I see . . . with my heart.

72

Looking at nothing, all of a sudden there it is! But the moment we see it, it disappears, leaving only a vague memory. (14)

We would love to live consistently in that state of awareness that comes from the sudden realization that "all is well and all will be well." When we experience that blissful state, we promise ourselves that we will hold on to it. We don't. Our mind insists that any new insight be quickly crammed into an existing box of cultural understandings and framed in a way that fits the "norm" of conditioned life.

- Jesus said that new wine cannot be put into old wineskins. If you want to be free, you must stop closing the prison door on yourself. How have you experienced tranquil awareness? What happened afterward?

Seeing or not . . . I know I belong.

73

Chasing after it is useless because it didn't begin anytime and isn't going anywhere. (14)

Chasing is another lovely conditioned process. We're like Wile E. Coyote, forever chasing the Road Runner with the aid of our culture's Acme products, and forever failing. Of course we must fail, for to succeed would bring the engine of culture to a grinding halt. We have built our world on striving and struggle to see another way of living.

- What are you chasing? Where have you looked for it? What we think we're chasing is everywhere, always. Stop, look, and listen.

No more . . . chasing.

74

We pay complete attention to whatever we are doing, as if we were crossing a river on ice-covered stones. (15)

We live in an attention-deficit world. No one takes the time to do just one thing at a time. No one has the patience to sit quietly without external stimuli. Thus, we are always slipping and falling into the freezing water. Oh, look! There goes a squirrel! *Splash.*

- What if every moment today is as important as that step onto a slippery stone in a river? Take your time. Make sure you're balanced.

I pay . . . complete attention.

75

We are alert to everything that happens, like a bird watching in all directions. (15)

When we are living in the flow of Tao, we can be watchful without being distracted. We expand our awareness of our environment without focusing on any one thing. It is a diffuse sort of awareness, just the opposite of selective, scattered attention. This broad awareness enables us to choose the most helpful place to put our attention, then return to awareness. Our attention isn't hijacked; rather, we remain in control of it.

- Let your senses expand to take in your environment without focusing on one thing in particular. Then pick something and focus on it. Then expand again. This is good practice.

First awareness . . . then attention.

76

We have a quiet dignity and reserve, like a guest who does not seek attention. (15)

Dignity and reserve are major casualties of our modern age. How many followers? How many "friends"? How many "likes"? We really believe that we must have more and more attention or we will not survive. That's the way the "game" is rigged. A person with essential dignity neither seeks nor needs attention.

- What would happen if you stopped playing the game? What would a life of true dignity look like?

I am a guest . . . of life.

77

There is a beautiful simplicity about us, like a gem before it is shaped and polished. (15)

Let's not spend another minute polishing our image. Let's not waste time grooming ourselves and presenting ourselves for the approval of other people. Let's dress simply. Let's speak quietly. Let's listen carefully and fully. Let's find out who and what we truly are and then live from that understanding.

- How might you present yourself in the most authentic fashion? No frills. No games. No bullshit.

Here . . . I am.

78

To notice this enlightenment, we sit patiently and wait for muddy thoughts to settle and our mind to become clear. Life then lives itself in us. (15)

Chasing enlightenment is futile. Trying to "find ourselves" is a never-ending task. Be very careful of becoming a "spiritual seeker." It sounds like a noble pursuit and has an air of sophistication about it, but it is really a waste of time. You are already what you seek. It is difficult to sit quietly and wait, but it is the only way to let life live within you.

- Sit quietly. Wait. Stop looking. See what's around you and act on that seeing.

Waiting . . . patiently.

79

Practicing this path, we no longer worry about what we have and don't have because we have everything. (15)

Advertising is always pointing out something we don't have that perhaps we should get. The Tao is always pointing out that we have enough. Advertising reminds us of what we lack. The Tao reminds us of what we have. Society fuels our worries. The Tao feeds our contentment. We will live until we die. In the meantime, why not enjoy ourselves?

- Make a list of everything you have. Is there really something else you actually need?

I have . . . everything.

80

When the chatter of our mind settles down, we find the still point. From this still point we watch everything come and go in perfect peace. (16)

The still point is always with us. Sometimes we ignore it because we want some external thing and actually keep ourselves agitated until we are able to get this thing that we want. This is a common process in this culture, but the peace we really want remains quietly waiting. When we live from this still point, we might want things and try to get things, but we also relax and watch them pass away. No problem.

- Being at peace and wanting something can coexist. But notice how the wanting has a different quality. What does it feel like?

Things come . . . things go.

81

Everything that is, was, or ever will be has a common source from which it comes, in which it lives, and to which it returns. (16)

Our belonging is deeper and more pervasive than we realize. From the point of view of the Tao, we have been a part of all that is since before the beginning of beginning-less time. In the Tao we live and breathe and have our being. All sense of separation is a tragic illusion, and authentic spiritual teachers from all traditions have consistently tried, using various images, to point this out.

- It is inevitable that you will often feel separate and at risk. Just remember, somewhere in the back of your mind, that this is an illusion, no matter how real it feels. When do you tend to feel separate?

I have always been . . . a part of Tao.

82

Understanding this coming and going, we return to our source and our confusion ends. (16)

Much of the confusion we experience is generated by our social structures. Society naturally attempts to bring order, security, and some sort of dependability to life. This is fine, but notice that the more we try to make things dependable, the more they slip into mystery and confusion. Only in our source will we find dependability.

- It is natural to be confused. Our minds cannot bring order to the ever-changing dance of life. When you let that confusion exist without undue effort to end it, it will fade.

Confusion . . . is natural.

83

Not understanding this, we remain confused and bring about great suffering. (16)

The constant attempts to impose security and dependability on life are exercises in futility. We can perhaps succeed for a brief moment, but then the whole thing twists away and we are left suffering because we feel we have failed. Notice how insecurity is viewed as failure by the conditioned outlook of society. Yet everything is transient and, by its nature, insecure. We wish it were different, but we don't have to suffer because it is not.

- Welcome your feelings of insecurity and let them introduce you to a deeper understanding of the Tao.

I am insecure . . . and that is fine.

84

Living at the still point, we are open to all of life. (16)

The further away from our center we are, the more we have to shut down our perceptions and guard our experiences. Away from the center, other people are seen as threats and events are seen as dangerous. When we are at our center, we do not feel threatened because we know we belong and are not truly at risk. This, of course, opens possibilities beyond our ordinary expectations.

- How self-protective are you in your life right now? What if you don't have to protect anything? How would you live?

The possibilities . . . are greater than I can imagine.

85

Open to all of life, we don't judge anything. (16)

When self-protection becomes a smaller part of life, we see events with greater clarity. We discern what might be helpful or unhelpful, but we don't dismiss ideas and people without thought. We allow ideas and people to be free to come and go; we don't need to protect ourselves from them.

- Think of the emotional energy you waste by trying to protect yourself from other people's ideas and opinions. How would this energy be better used?

No need . . . to waste my energy.

86

Not judging, we see with compassion. (16)

Compassion is a natural quality of our human existence. It does not have to be generated but can be discovered waiting beneath our conditioned judgments and fears. As we learn to let our fearful judgments fade away, we will find that compassion is our natural attitude toward all of life. It will express itself in ways appropriate to our situations.

- You don't have to try to be compassionate. Just notice what fears, opinions, and judgments exist. When they are gone, compassion is there.

My true nature . . . is compassion.

87

Seeing with compassion, we discover our true nature. Discovering our true nature, we are at home and nothing in life disturbs us. (16)

Remember that our true nature is perfectly at home in life. It doesn't fret about security. It doesn't try to control. It knows that it belongs and is able to take action with effectiveness but without strain. It dances with changes with grace and ease. It lives fully and dies peacefully, knowing that all things are unfolding as they should.

- It is all about discovering who you really are. All the words in the *Tao Te Ching* are merely pointing to this discovery. Once you understand who you really are, you can stop worrying and simply live undisturbed.

I am . . . undisturbed.

88

The deepest virtue is to be unaware of a separate self at all. (17)

The conditioned mind will always feel separate because it is a mechanism of the physical brain. On those rare moments when our brain stops thinking about itself, we are truly at home and at peace. This is the place of our deepest power and natural virtue. We are, at these moments, who and what we were truly meant to be and our power is immense. Our compassion is without limit.

- Your ego will always feel itself to be separate. It is part of you, but it is not critical to your existence. It can be a tiny fraction of your experience of life. You don't have to fight it, but can you let it become less and less in charge?

I am not . . . an ego.

89

Being aware of a separate self, it is good to have compassion for that self. (17)

Because we are all almost constantly identified by a separate ego, there is no use feeling guilty or bad about it. It is just the way we have learned to see ourselves. The ego, in all its different masks or personas, always suffers. It is always, to some degree, afraid. It always struggles for security and stability. Poor thing. It suffers from "delusions of identity." It was not designed to carry such a load, and it is good to notice that our true nature has nothing but compassion for it.

- How are you punishing yourself? Self-punishment is a sure way of keeping the ego in place. Lighten up on yourself.

Poor ego . . . be at rest.

90

Not having compassion for our self, we become afraid of our own nature. (17)

Many paths of spiritual exploration hit a dead end when the ego becomes terrified of giving up its role as our "identity." Our spiritual path then begins to circle around known and comfortable beliefs and assumptions. We think we are making spiritual progress when we are actually treading water. We then punish ourselves, which only serves to keep us stuck. As long as we are punishing the ego, it gets to keep existing and calling the shots.

- Self-punishment only serves to ensure that there will always be a self (ego) to punish. What would happen if you stopped the punishment?

Never a need . . . to punish.

91

Being afraid of our own nature, we come to actually hate our self. Hating our self, how can we value anyone else? (17)

Fear is the energy that fuels the engine of hate. Look around. See the way hate permeates our culture. Notice how it begins with fear, then goes to blame, then proceeds on to hate. Make no mistake, any hatred we feel is, at the root, self-hatred. Remember that this is really one part of our ego hating the other parts in a vicious circle.

- What would happen if you stopped hating yourself? How can self-acceptance flow out toward others?

Poor ego . . . be gentle and still.

92

Free from self-hate, our actions are not burdened by the need for attention. Therefore, people say, "It happened naturally." (17)

This is how wu wei becomes free to guide our actions. The ego-selves are put aside for a time and the natural self does the work. Because there is no ego reference operating, there is no "one" who needs the attention, no "one" who is judging the actions. We look at "our" accomplishments with joy, and when someone compliments us, we think, "It wasn't really me that did it."

- Of course it feels good to accomplish something. But notice that the greatest satisfaction arises when there is little, if any, ego involvement. It simply happened.

Thank you . . . but it happened by itself.

93

When we forget who we truly are, we turn to external rules to define goodness and morality. (18)

Concepts such as goodness and morality too easily become defined by rules of behavior. A "good" person will act in this way. It is "immoral" to act some other way. These rules may be helpful guidelines as we grow from childhood and learn how to apply our intrinsic goodness in specific situations, but they are not intrinsic goodness itself.

- How does it feel to think of rules as simply guidelines? It can be threatening, especially if you've believed the rule for decades. Rules are not the same as your intrinsic goodness.

Deep within me . . . is goodness.

94

When we no longer live from our heart, we look for clever strategies to guide our actions. (18)

We seem to value cleverness more than heartfelt honesty, don't we? Scheming and plotting often replace straightforward open actions. Do we really need to be Machiavellian in our strategies for living? If we are conditioned to see daily life as a battle, then we will surely make it into one, playing into the hands of competition. The mind battles. The heart relaxes.

- Notice the ways you tense your thoughts and your body throughout the day. If life is a battle for you, perhaps you are in the wrong line of work.

I am not . . . at war with life.

95

Duty and loyalty become substitutes for our inability to love ourselves and others. (18)

If we were living according to our true nature, no one would have to use words like *duty* and *loyalty.* We would act for the good of all without a second thought. But because we feel so separate from life, we demand things like loyalty oaths in an effort to control people. We use the word *duty* to mean doing something we really don't want to do. Our true nature does what is good without the need for force.

- Let yourself feel pleasure at things your mind wants to call "duty." Remember such actions are natural.

I naturally . . . do what's right.

96

We insist our leaders heal the suffering created by our own divided minds. (18)

Politics is really just passing the buck, isn't it? Candidates promise to fix the things that we have all cooperated in fouling up. We think that voting is all the responsibility we need to take. Then we wonder why nothing ever changes. Political life as we know it would cease to exist if we each took personal responsibility for our place in life. We would naturally care for the community without the need for laws. Idealistic, yes, but good to keep in mind when we begin to get drawn into the political morass.

- What are you looking for elected leaders to fix? What can you do about it?

I am . . . responsible.

97

If we give up our attempts to be holy and wise, everyone, including ourselves, will benefit. (19)

Seeking to be holy and wise will never bring true holiness and wisdom. Only the conditioned mind seeks these things. Our true nature is holy and wise simply because that is its inherent state. Holiness is akin to "whole-ness"—the act of being fully who and what we truly are. The external ideas of holiness and wisdom actually interfere with our wholeness.

- Can you see yourself as "holy and wise"? What resistance arises to that thought?

I am holy . . . and wise.

98

If we give up our rules for goodness and justice, all beings will naturally be treated with loving-kindness. (19)

Kindness can never be legislated. It can only be nurtured and cultivated. Justice can never be achieved by rule of law. It can only be found in compassionate hearts. The Taoism of Lao-tzu is quite anarchistic and frightening to those of us who are conditioned to believe that only by force of law will people behave. How well has this worked for us? Laws may be necessary, but let's not mistake them for an actual solution to our society's ills.

- If there were no laws governing your behavior, would you act with honor and compassion? Don't bring up your worries about other people. How would *you* act?

I am by nature . . . good and just.

99

If we give up trying to accumulate by clever means, theft will disappear. (19)

Lao-tzu speaks in idealist terms in order to force us to see things from a new perspective. Why would a person steal if there was no drive to accumulate? Why would a person cheat if no one cared about power and influence? Theft can only exist where there is fear that there will not be enough. When a land is content with simple pleasures, no one needs to lock their doors.

- Have you ever stolen or cheated? No punishment here, just look at the honest reasons why.

I have no need . . . to accumulate.

100

The core of our path is this: we see through our conditioned mind and find our true nature waiting. (19)

All our striving to be secure, to be good, and to be worthy is the work of our conditioning. Underneath these conditioned impulses, we are beings who do not need to strive. We are people whose nature is goodness. We are of inestimable worth simply because we are part of the Whole, the Tao. All the teachings of the *Tao Te Ching* are just ways of reminding us of this fact.

- What if you really, truly, deep down believed that you were secure, good, and worthy no matter what? How would your life change?

I truly am . . . good and worthy.

101

We always strive to make the right choice and always fear the wrong choice. (20)

Choices are framed by our conditioned mind as binary. They are either right or wrong. This puts enormous pressure on us and actually inhibits our ability to make helpful choices. Choices are never binary. They are always nuanced and contain hidden assumptions and perspectives that we will see only when we relax and let go of our fears. One choice always leads to another in an unfathomable, unfolding pathway.

- As you face a current choice, consider whether you have allowed yourself to see things that are hidden and not obvious to your conditioned mind.

I can choose . . . without fear.

102

We pursue what others say is good and avoid what others say is bad. How sad this is for us. (20)

Most of us reach adulthood with certain categories firmly implanted in our conditioned mind. We may consider ourselves free to take whatever path we want, but, in fact, we are usually guided by unconscious ideas that reflect the consensus of society. It is very difficult to notice this unconscious force and even more difficult to act contrary to it. Conditioning is a powerful force and should not be underestimated.

- Are you taking the path in life that you truly believe is good, true, and authentic for your soul?

Help me . . . be an authentic soul.

103

People are constantly stirred up like children at a circus—always looking for the next act to entertain them. But this practice asks us to remain undisturbed and watch all things with the detached interest of a newborn. (20)

It is the constant stir of society and media that keeps us off-balance. There is a certain energy in the constant hit of entertainment that is terribly addictive. The kind of serenity and wisdom that comes from not being identified with all the stir is seldom experienced. Something inside our brain gets addicted to stimulation, not serenity; entertainment, not wisdom; control, not release.

- Are you able to have moments of detachment? What are the benefits of sometimes being detached? What are the difficulties?

Help me . . . watch and see.

104

In a culture where excess accumulation is the norm, this path seems idiotic. Fearful voices in our mind warn us that we will end up wandering the street, homeless and alone. (20)

Deep within we long for a simple joy of just being alive, but the illusion of separation from the Divine keeps us in a constant state of unconscious fear and distrust. We are taught that the only way to ease this fear is to continually amass the things that promise to keep us secure. Sometimes it works. But even when it seems to fulfill its promise, something still remains beneath the surface that makes us wonder.

- What if you ended up poor and alone? Could you find a way to be at peace? If so, you have understood the essence of this path.

I can be at peace . . . regardless.

105

This practice asks us to relinquish the illusion of control and to be content with whatever comes our way. This seems so strange and different from the usual way, but it is the way of life itself. (20)

Three authentic spiritual teachers have preached trust, acceptance, and contentment with whatever comes our way—Lao-tzu, the Buddha, and Jesus. We still don't believe them. We still look for loopholes, exceptions, and misunderstandings. "They didn't really mean . . ." We continue to fear the idea of radical trust. But only radical trust will open the door to an effective, joyous, and creative life. Only radical trust will free us to live.

- What fear holds you back from practicing radical trust?

Help me . . . to trust.

106

Though this way seems elusive and avoids our words and concepts, it is the source of everything, seen and unseen. (21)

It has to be elusive. If we could pin it down with an idea or a belief, we would then think that we could control it. We would place it in a category of study and pretend we knew what we were talking about. Instead, we have to let words and concepts sit lightly in our mind. All the things we see and all the mysteries we cannot see are safe beyond our illusions of control.

- Isn't it a freeing feeling to know you can't control this path? The Tao is beyond all that. Just for today, let go of the need to know or to control—anything.

I am free . . . to know nothing.

107

Though walking this path seems to take us into deep and hidden shadows, it leads us into the very life force of all things. (21)

As we walk along this path, we will experience the occasional "dark night." Everything we thought we knew will seem foolish and we will feel lost and alone. This is normal, even essential. We must feel foolish at times in order to drop false ego and pride. We must feel lost at times or we will delude ourselves that we are in charge.

- Don't fear the lost feelings. Don't despair when you can't get a grip on things. You are still on the path and you're never alone.

I am never lost . . . never alone.

108

Since before the beginning of beginningless time, it has been both creator of and witness to all existence. (21)

There is only one possible path. To each person it has unique characteristics, obstacles, and scenery and thus it seems we are on different paths. However, it is one path, one Way, that encompasses the entire cosmos, seen and unseen. We can enjoy our journey and let other people enjoy theirs.

- Pay attention today to how the Tao is unfolding for you in a unique manner. Don't worry about whether you are doing it "right" or "wrong."

I am . . . on my way.

109

We know the truth of this way, not by believing it but by being it. (21)

There are no beliefs you have to create and cling to. You only have to notice what is happening and use everything in your experience to inform you about yourself and your life. You are not being punished, nor are you being rewarded. You are simply having the opportunity to feel what it is like to be alive in this moment, in this place.

- If you try to make sense out of it, you will fail. Let go of that effort. Just breathe, feel, touch, taste, laugh, and cry. You *are* the answer.

I am . . . the answer to my questions.

110

Accepting what is, we find it to be perfect. What seemed distorted is seen as true. What seemed lacking is seen as abundant. What seemed worn out is seen as fresh and new. (22)

No one is asking that we pretend that suffering, pain, loss, and injustice are not to be addressed and alleviated however possible. We are being asked to accept that what is happening . . . is what is happening. We are then asked to look ever more deeply into this "what is" and see how it contains the seeds of transformation within it. Nurturing these seeds is our work—our perfect work, our perfect life.

- Look deeply into the "is-ness" of the life you experience. You want the perfect job for your life? Here it is.

My life is perfectly . . . what it is.

111

Possessing little, we are content. Too much stuff and we lose our way. (22)

Lao-tzu repeats this truth again and again because no one wants to hear it. No one wants to believe it. The life of simple joys is the life our souls were meant to have. We have pretended that satisfaction and happiness are qualities that can be bought and stored in our ever bigger houses. It. Will. Never. Work. How many times do we need to hear this truth?

- Simplify your life. It will be a difficult task because you will find no encouragement from your conditioned mind or your conditioned society. Do it anyway. Choose simplicity today.

I am simply . . . content.

112

When we reside at our center, our actions nurture all things. We don't act out of ego needs, so our actions are enlightened. (22)

Wu wei, effortless action, cannot be faked. We are either letting the Tao flow through us and live as us, or we are separating ourselves from life, making ourselves and others miserable, and ultimately causing harm. If we are still and quiet, living from something deep within us, we will be truly doing life's work. We don't have to try so hard. Really.

- Stop trying to have your own way. Stop trying to fix yourself and others. Let go and do what comes naturally in each moment and you will wake up and enjoy life.

I let the Tao . . . live my life.

113

We don't claim to be perfect, so our ideas are welcomed. We aren't looking for reward, so our teaching is enduring and accessible to all. We don't try to control or convince anyone, so opposition is not an issue. (22)

We are not dispensing advice from high ground. We are not making grand pronouncements about what people should believe. We aren't telling them what they should do. We aren't asking for anything from them. We are not being arrogant or condescending. We are simply trying to live in compassion for all beings. We are willing to help however we can. This makes our work effective.

- Examine your words and actions to see what elements of superiority, arrogance, pride, and hubris you might be communicating. Drop them.

I simply . . . want to help.

114

"Accept what is and find it to be perfect" is not an idle phrase. Acceptance of life is the only path to wholeness. (22)

Remember that acceptance is not the same as resignation. Acceptance is simply a clear, honest awareness of what is really going on. You see through the BS—your own and that of other people. Only when the BS is cleared away and our own fantasies, wishes, and wants are courageously laid aside will we see the way ahead. And that way is truly a way of joy and creative satisfaction.

- Are you accepting the life you have before you? Really? How are you fooling yourself?

I want . . . to accept.

115

This is a path of few words. Silence is the natural way of life. (23)

Silence of the voice. Silence of the mind. Only in these silences can we find the way we seek. Words of philosophy will not do it. Religious preaching will not do it. Doctrines and beliefs may abound, but they are useless. Is it any wonder our culture feels adrift? We are lost in a sea of noise, signifying nothing.

- Be quiet. Hear it again: Be quiet!

I come . . . to the quiet.

116

Strong winds arise, and pass away.
Torrential rains arise, and pass away.
Even the cosmos, which produces
the wind and the rain, passes away.
Why, then, so much concern over
what to do and what to say? (23)

It is all a matter of perspective, isn't it? Everything is transient, yet we spend so much of our energy trying to convince ourselves of permanence. A short one hundred years from now who will care about the self-generated dramas we take with so much solemnity? Some grandchildren may have a vague memory of us, but give it another one hundred years. Relax!

- Imagine the world seventy-five years from now. Are you still here? What is all the fuss?

I come . . . and I go . . . and that . . . is fine.

117

Our life is an expression of life itself. Our true nature expresses itself in everything we do. (23)

We are who and what we are. Accepting that is essential to a contented life. We make mistakes and that is part of what is. We may make horrendous mistakes, and they, too, become a part of the Whole that will be woven with compassion into the cosmos. Underneath our mistakes remains our true nature, always able to understand, to act, and to heal even when we are unaware of its work.

- You can accept the whole of your life because it is not what your ego-conditioned mind tells you it is. It is deeper than all that.

I may do harm . . . I work to heal that harm.

118

Success and failure are seen as part of a seamless, joyful whole. Each is accepted and fully lived. (23)

Fully living our failures is difficult. We would rather ignore them, push them into the background, excuse them, justify them, and in general refuse to work with them to gain insight and understanding in our lives. Or we spend our lives reliving and regretting them. We really don't have to avoid them or be afraid of them. They are part of the wondrous tapestry of our lives.

- Stop ignoring your mistakes. Also stop obsessing over them. Just let them be part of the amazing life you have been given.

I am not . . . my mistakes.

119

Stretching to reach it, we fall. Running to catch it, we get lost. (24)

We are not really "spiritual seekers." To seek implies that we are missing something we somehow need. The same is true with the idea of "running after" something. The seeking and the running keep us distracted and unable to see the plain obvious fact: *we already have that which we are trying to find.* We have always had it and always will.

- Stop and take a breath. Your practice is that of finding yourself in each and every moment to be fully at home and safe within the Tao (God, Source, Mystery).

I am always . . . at home.

120

Pretending to be enlightened, we become dim and foolish. Trying to "do it right," we fail. (24)

A spiritual path is not something that needs to be done "right." We don't have to pretend—that is, we don't have to act holy and wise. No one needs our masquerades and holy personas. A spiritual path is a quiet path of paying attention, of learning how we interpret and misinterpret things that happen, of becoming more and more at home as ourselves without artifice and cunning.

- You do, in a sense, make progress along your path. You understand yourself more and more each day. When you stop pretending, you see clearly, and . . . amazingly . . . you change.

No need . . . to pretend.

121

Looking for praise, we receive nothing. (24)

Our conditioned mind is looking for reinforcement at every turn. It will even take our spiritual practice and turn it outward in a subtle display: "See how spiritual I am. I'm not like an ordinary person. My spiritual life is much deeper and more sophisticated . . . and humble." It is ever so subtle and insidious.

- When you talk about your path, remember that praise is only for the conditioned mind. Share your true nature, not your conditioned mind.

I look for . . . nothing.

122

Grabbing hold of it, we lose it. (24)

Grabbing hold of something implies control of that something. Our conditioned mind is frightened of open-ended living. It wants our path to give us answers that can be pinned down and written in holy books. It wants to create theologies and philosophies that can be analyzed and have PhD theses written about them. Beware of "ologies."

- Take care as you study books, including this one. You can't pin down the things you want to pin down. There is no controlling this path.

I hold my path . . . in open hands.

123

All of this strutting, striving, straining, and grasping is excess baggage. The very freedom it promises does not appear until we lay it down. (24)

We are reminded constantly that our path is one of simplicity and humility. We are not "becoming spiritual." We are becoming ourselves—our true selves. We carry so much extra baggage in every other area of life, why would we want to add more in the name of spirituality? We will learn eventually to lay every bit of it down and walk with lightness and freedom.

- Practice a laying-down exercise daily. Pick up a book, look at it a moment, then lay it down. Pick it up. Lay it down.

I pick things up . . . and lay them down, carrying nothing.

124

The path we follow existed before the universe was born. It contains within itself unchanging tranquility and solitude. (25)

We and the path we walk are integral to the fabric of the cosmos. We are not strangers here and are never truly lost. Deep within us, we find a place of true belonging. It is a place of solitude, but not of loneliness. It is a place where we find that everything we need is part of our very nature. We are not anxious seekers. We are tranquil finders.

- In one sense, you must walk this path by yourself. In another sense, you belong to the Whole. Notice both the feelings of being alone and of belonging. Integrate the two.

I am alone . . . I am not alone.

125

It is present wherever we turn and provides inexhaustible compassion to all beings. Thus, it may be considered the Mother of the universe. (25)

The feminine principle of nurture and acceptance is central to Lao-tzu's image of the Tao. The compassion revealed is not the sentimental coddling of the overindulgent mother. It is the sharp, honest, and direct expression of caring by an energy that understands all and works for the good of all. It encompasses every possible experience that life brings and provides a core of strength to all beings as they navigate their way.

- Don't look for a sentimental "good mother" figure who will rescue you from responsibility and protect you from pain. Look for a powerful Goddess who provides inexhaustible power and strength.

I can trust . . . the mother of all.

126

It has no name, but if we have to refer to it, we call it Tao. It can also be called the great mystery from which we come, in which we live, and to which we return. (25)

Remember that the word *Tao* is nothing more than a metaphorical representation of that which cannot be named. When asked about how a "Taoist" would act, I cannot respond because there really is no such thing. We are all pilgrims along the "Way" of life in which each moment takes us around the great circle of coming and returning.

- You don't have to believe in the Tao any more than you believe in gravity. It simply is, and the wise life seeks to understand it and act according to it.

I come . . . I live . . . I return.

127

It is a path filled with grandeur of the cosmos, the earth, and the human heart. (25)

In Lao-tzu's mind these three elements, the cosmos, the earth, and the human heart, are connected in an inseparable manner. Each reflects a particular wondrous facet of the Mystery. The cosmos, mysterious and grand as it is, must express itself in the life of Earth and in the consciousness of the human soul. Nothing is an accident. Everything is necessary.

- You are necessary. The fact that you are here indicates that the "Whole Thing" needs you in order to exist as it does. Remove you, and like a Jenga tower, it all falls apart.

I am . . . necessary.

128

This path is our true home because it is home to all things in heaven and on earth. (25)

It feels like we are homesteading, carving out a place for ourselves from a wilderness. But our home is not a separate place, distanced from the dance of the infinite universe. It is nestled among this endless array of beings, forms, and manifestations. Once again we find that our hidden longing to belong, really belong, is satisfied completely by the nature of the Tao.

- Work to build your life and your home, but remember that you have never left, and never will leave, your true home.

I am . . . always at home.

129

Because this path is deeply rooted, it allows us to be lighthearted and not take ourselves too seriously. (26)

The depth of our soul's home within the Tao is a fundamental understanding that allows life to have, even at the hardest moments, a sense of play—not a trivial playing but an awareness that all this drama will pass away one day, and we will go home again—perhaps to play a new game in the morning.

- You are a spiritual being, born in and contained in the Tao. You are having an embodied experience. Savor it. Don't be overly somber about it.

I am . . . at play in a great Game.

130

Because this path is stable, it allows us to act without rashness. So, whatever we do, we do not abandon ourselves. (26)

Even when it feels like your feet are on shifting sand, remember that you are safe. Don't panic and act without thinking just because you feel desperate. Stay in touch with your soul, your heart, that part of you that is eternally with the Tao. That part will know what best to do in each moment. It won't panic and run in circles. It is there for us.

- Don't panic. Don't grasp at the nearest solution in desperation. Remember who and what you are. Act from that.

I will not . . . panic.

131

Even though the world supplies endless worries and distractions, we remain unconcerned and content. We have everything we could want. (26)

Remaining content amid the never-ending barrage of media that stimulates the twin demons of fear and desire requires a great deal of willingness. Willingness, remember, is the key to awakening. We must be willing to admit that we are addicts, hooked on the energetic stimulation that fear and desire create. When we are willing to drop our addictions, everything is waiting for us.

- The key to knowing whether you are dependent on something is to see if you can give it up for thirty days. Can you go thirty days without trivial media or unnecessary purchases?

My addictions . . . keep me trapped.

132

We have everything we could want. Why would we scurry about looking for something else? Only if we lose touch with our true nature are we trapped by agitation and hurry. (26)

Living under the leadership of our conditioned mind, we will always be driven, looking, stressing, and striving. When we begin to submit to our true nature, we stop the hurry. We stop striving for more. We act with the effortlessness and effectiveness of a flowing river. It is always our choice, in every moment, as to which we follow.

- Don't fool yourself. Every moment is a choice. Who will you follow? Your conditioned habits or your deeper true nature?

At this moment . . . I choose my true nature.

133

This path has no rules, no rituals, and no preconceived notions. (27)

We follow only one guideline. It is not a commandment. It is not set in stone or in a holy book. We are not punished if we do not follow it. It is simply this: we will use everything in our experience to see how we habitually follow our conditioned mind so we can drop that and return to our true selves.

- Each moment is an opportunity to see how you make yourself miserable. All you have to do is drop it. No punishment. Every moment is a new opportunity.

I see . . . I drop it . . . I come home.

134

Everything that happens is for our benefit. Everything in our experience instructs us in the way. (27)

The Tao does not send pain and loss. Our lives are transient, and loss and grief are part of the package. Events are never sent as punishment or to teach us a lesson—but—it is always our choice as to how we will respond to whatever happens, always. We hold that power in our hands—benefit or harm? What shall we make of things? Benefit or harm?

- What are you making of the events of your life right now?

Benefit . . . or harm?

135

Everyone we meet becomes our teacher, good and bad alike. Everyone we meet becomes our student, bright and dull alike. (27)

If we pay attention, each encounter in each and every moment teaches us something about what life is about: beauty, compassion, acceptance, wonder, loss, grief, wisdom, and endless qualities of the good life. Of course, each encounter also teaches those around us, and ourselves, something about us.

- Are you open to being taught in every encounter? What are you teaching at the same time?

I am a student . . . I am a teacher.

136

If we try to pick and choose, we will never learn. Ceasing to pick and choose: this is the great secret of life. (27)

There is a process called "confirmation bias." It is the way we tend to select the things we view, read, and listen to according to our preconceived ideas. We unconsciously filter out contrary information, people, and thoughts—ending up creating a cozy little world of only like-minded people. This can keep us captivated, gullible, and ready to consume whatever fits into our narrowed worldview at the moment.

- Be careful of how you choose what you watch, hear, and read. Avoid both the irritating and the comforting. Don't believe either what "they" say or what you think.

I let things be . . . just what they are.

137

Striving to make our way in the world seems prudent. But if we trust our heart, we may find the way opening with the effortless ease of a budding flower. (28)

The idea of "making our way" is deeply conditioned in our minds. We have to "make" a living rather than simply living. And it does seem prudent, doesn't it? After all, no one is going to just hand us food and shelter. But it is the addition of striving that separates it from the Tao. Our work is naturally going to meet our simple needs when it is chosen in accordance with our heart and with the needs of the community.

- What went into your choice of work? Does it feel natural and effortless?

I put aside my striving . . . and I trust.

138

Striving to live a life of virtue is approved by all. But if we trust our heart, we may find the power of our true nature everywhere we turn, in everyone we meet. (28)

Living our life for the approval of others is a misery. We pretend we are being good and virtuous, but we are really just striving for the acceptance and validation of the external world. True virtue is an innate quality within our very being. It doesn't look for approval or think of goodness. It simply does what is natural whether the world approves or not.

- Are you looking for approval? From whom? Why? Does it stop you from doing what you know, deep down, is right?

My virtue . . . is hidden within me.

139

Charismatic personalities capture our attention. But it is our true nature, existing beneath our personality, that brings power and purpose to our life. (28)

The word *personality* derives from the Greek word *persona*, meaning "mask." We create and modify our personality to get what we think we need from other people. The more carefully and skillfully we craft these masks, the more attention the world gives us. But they are just masks. They are not real.

- Who are you? Don't answer with reference to a personality, a mask. Who are you, really?

I am not . . . my personalities.

140

Separate from our true nature, we create forms and functions and struggle to make them work. Returning to our original nature, we use the forms and functions for the benefit of all. (28)

All our inventions, creations, buildings, societies, beliefs, toys, and trinkets are simply forms. They are not necessarily bad, but they seldom meet the expectations we have for them. When they emerge from our conditioned mind, they don't fit with the nature of things and can cause unexpected harm. When they emerge from our deeper Tao mind, they merge smoothly with things and become beneficial.

- Are the things I do of benefit to people? Why do I do the things I do?

I work . . . to benefit all.

141

Attempting to control external events will never keep us safe. Control is an illusion. (29)

It is natural for us to take action in the world and try to arrange things so we will feel safe. Notice, however, that we never, ever feel entirely safe because something can always occur that is outside of our ability to control. If we realize this truth, our actions will be more effective, not attempting to do the impossible.

- There is nothing wrong with taking action, but you will be happier when you admit that you can't really control life.

I act . . . but can't control.

142

Whatever we try to control we separate from ourselves. (29)

There are various insidious ways of controlling people by playing to their fears and desires. Our culture is particularly skilled at this process. Notice, however, how this treats human beings as objects, things to be manipulated and used for our own benefit. We may seem to control others—our children, our spouse, our employees—but what we think we gain is a tragic illusion.

- Who are you trying to control? How? What if you stopped?

I will not . . . control you.

143

Whatever we try to fix we ruin. (29)

We are told that we should make the world a better place. But do we actually know what "better" is? When we try to make something better, we stop seeing it clearly and see instead our image of how it should be. When we stop trying to fix it, we see it clearly. When we see it clearly, we can act in helpful ways.

- What are you trying to fix? That's not necessarily bad, but are you seeing it clearly first?

I see clearly . . . before I act.

144

We return to our breathing. It knows exactly what to do, rising and falling without conscious control. In the same way we sometimes have an excess and sometimes have a lack. We sometimes assert ourselves and sometimes hold back. We sometimes succeed and sometimes fail completely. Our practice is to see all this without abandoning ourselves. (29)

"Sustainable growth" is an oxymoron. Growth can never be sustained. Having must give way to losing or there will be no room to have again. Living must give way to dying or there will be no room to live again. Success will eventually lead to failure, which will lead once again to success. This is the necessary rhythm of life.

- Let the yin/yang circling of life take its course without taking it personally. Flow with it and use it for benefit.

I succeed . . . I fail . . . I succeed again.

145

Practicing this path, we do not struggle. To struggle is to invite resistance. To invite resistance is to create suffering, in our life and in the world. (30)

Our struggles are often semi-hidden. We're only vaguely aware that we are struggling. Our muscles are taut, our jaw is tight, and our stomach rumbles. Why does life seem so difficult? Because we are bringing square pegs to round holes with almost every thought we have. We pound and pound. Even if we get it to fit, look at the damage we've done.

- Ask yourself why you feel stressed. Square peg? Round hole?

Only what is mine to do . . . I do.

146

Paying attention to the present moment, we see the things we must do. We do them without complaint, resistance, or second-guessing, then we stop. (30)

Matching the shape of our pegs to the holes the Tao is providing at the moment requires wisdom and nonresistance. We can then exert a great deal of energy, but it will be energy that fits the task at hand. Thus, it is effective. We do no damage and contribute to a good life for all.

- What things do you do that create resistance? Can you go through the day steadily and conscientiously and still not force things?

I have . . . no need to force.

147

We don't complicate our actions by seeking control or recognition. (30)

Often, when we work at multiple tasks and have many interactions with people throughout the day, we come home and replay it all. Every conversation and presentation gets paraded before a panel of judges with scorecards at the ready. We think of things we should or should not have said. No wonder we are still tired the next day.

- There's no need to spend more than five minutes, if that, in review of the day. Perhaps review it once, no more. The past is beyond your control—release it!

When the day is over . . . it is over.

148

Correct action, however difficult, is naturally focused and effective. (30)

Wu wei, the flowing nature of correct action, does not mean that we don't face difficulties, roadblocks, and intense work. It just means that we are not adding to the difficulty by our own needs to fix, control, win, succeed, et cetera. Imagine the work of a good professional athlete—hard, intense work, but also play and joy.

- Are you functioning like an athlete? Not just sports, but life?

My day . . . is my play.

149

Struggle complicates and does not lead to lasting good. (30)

Why all the fuss? Rivers carve beds, but the beds are not the river. Whatever we force into our lives—all the accomplishments, acquisitions, and honors—will die with our bodies. Whatever we allow to flow through us will remain forever a part of the Tao. We are not the riverbed, not the things that we've created. We are the river.

- Let your actions flow in, then out again. That way they will last eternally.

I do my work . . . then let it go.

150

Weapons of violence are contrary to the common good, no matter how skillfully used. Therefore, we vow to do no harm. (31)

A massive defense budget and drones that kill from a faraway safe distance are complemented by nukes that lie in wait to cleanse the earth. At a gun show we can buy armor-piercing shells for our own use. These things keep us "safe" while we huddle in our dens and watch violence of all kinds play out on our screens.

- What weapons do you own? Why?

I vow . . . to do no harm.

151

Faced with unavoidable violence, we remember this vow, act quickly, and return immediately to peace. (31)

Lao-tzu was not a doctrinaire pacifist. He understood the possible necessity of defensive action but urged that such action bring a minimum amount of harm and be followed quickly by actions that lessened resentment and brought reconciliation. Keeping in mind the importance of reconciliation, we might be better at avoiding violence in the first place.

- Are you holding resentments that could trigger violence? Can you head that violence off?

After violence . . . I offer healing.

152

Battles are not with "enemies" but with human beings like ourselves. (31)

It seems insane to think that another human being would see us as an enemy, yet many around the world do just that. It seems insane that we would fear these people, but we do. These impulses exist entirely within our brains, yet these electrochemical signals can ignite a flame that could kill millions. The battlefield is the images within our minds. This is where we must do our battles.

- Your work for peace begins within your mind. How will you do that work?

My enemy . . . is like me. We are both . . . afraid.

153

We do not rejoice in victory nor take delight in the downfall of others. (31)

The idea of "We're number one!" pervades our culture. We think that "kicking butt and taking names" is the way to thrive in business. Winning and losing have become the measuring sticks for life. This is contrary to the Tao. We should take care with victory parades.

- Notice your own feelings about "victory" in sports and other competitions. Do you see the violence and hatred toward the "other" team not far beneath the surface?

I seek to conquer . . . only my own conditioned mind.

154

Victory is an illusion that gains us nothing. Once a battle is over, we lay our weapons down and weep that this has happened. (31)

The young men and women who serve in our armed forces are beautiful beings. They all have warm hearts and kindness behind their eyes. They are deployed to war zones on a tragically regular basis. We are proud of their capacity and courage, but we weep for the world that makes young men and women dress in uniforms and be ordered to kill for old men in suits and ties. The sacrifice of veterans is far deeper than any Veterans Day can mark.

- Have you ever cried over what we as humans have done? Why not?

I weep . . . for all of us.

155

What we call the Tao really has no name. Naming something, we think we understand it. What we call the Tao is far too subtle for that. (32)

To our conditioned minds, everything has a name. Everything is identified and placed in a category. This is the foundation of science and has brought us many blessings. Even science, however, bows before that which it cannot contain with its categories. We can't conceive of the "nameless." Even the word *nameless* is a name.

- Let your mind think of "no-thing." Impossible. But that's the Tao.

I can't . . . imagine.

156

If we hold on to our true nature, all external and internal strife falls away. Peace descends on our life like a gentle rain from heaven. Joy flows from the earth like a mighty river. (32)

It may be only for a brief moment, but we sometimes glimpse that inexpressible assurance that all is well. Our conditioned mind quickly steps in to remind us that, no, all is not well, and then trots out its many examples proving its point. But the memory of assurance remains in the center of who we truly are. We remember it when life's chaos closes in and it becomes a place to plant our feet.

- Take a deep breath. Inside of you is a place of true peace. Feel it for a moment.

Peace is . . . in my heart.

157

There is no need to urge ourselves to do good. Goodness is our heart's true nature. (32)

Lao-tzu repeats this over and over. Stop trying to do good. We're trying to please our parents, our teachers, our boss, and our own conditioned minds. We don't have to do that. When we accept that we *are* good, natural goodness flows through us. Without the pressure of trying to please, we find a wonderful freedom of action.

- Believe it. Inside of you, hidden by decades of conditioned thinking, is the fundamental desire to be of good service to life.

My natural goodness . . . is waiting to flow.

158

The more we use words, the more distinctions we make. The more distinctions we make, the more we suffer. (32)

There is only One Thing Happening. It manifests in infinite forms and it is sometimes helpful to explore how these many intriguing forms interact and work together, but it's just One Thing Happening. We are one of these infinite forms, just as a cell in our body is one of the millions of forms within us.

- You are just one form in a universe of infinite forms. Be yourself.

I am one part . . . of an infinite Life.

159

We return to peace just as streams and rivers return to the ocean. (32)

The water falling from the sky will end up in the ocean, one way or another. So it flows in streams, fills lakes, tumbles over cliffs, evaporates, and rains again . . . never doubting that it will reach home. And once home in the ocean, it waits to evaporate into the clouds and rain once again. We are made of the same energy as that water.

- Wherever you are right now, don't doubt for a moment that you will return home.

I will . . . return to peace.

160

Studying other people brings us knowledge. Studying our own mind brings us freedom. (33)

Without a deep understanding of our own nature, we are defined by other people's ideas of us. Self-awareness is quite different from self-absorption. Self-absorption is being lost in the images and masks of our personality. Self-awareness is an observation of all these different masks and an understanding of how to see through them.

- Who are you? A question to repeat often because it's too easy to give a conditioned answer.

I am not . . . who I think I am.

161

Overcoming other people requires force. Overcoming our conditioning requires true power. (33)

People struggling for freedom will make any sacrifice for their cause. They will fight and kill and die to escape being controlled by others. Yet they never even notice the controlling voice inside that orders them around, enslaving the "free" person with unseen bars made of thoughts and ideas.

- If you would be truly free, you must overcome the internal assumptions and ideas that are your unseen oppressors.

I seek freedom . . . from my own mind.

162

Once we realize that we always have everything we need, we understand that we are truly adequate for our life. (33)

Enough seems a dirty word in a culture that insists there is always more to get, have, and make ours. The economy is founded on the never-ending accumulation of trinkets. Striving to continue to accumulate is built into our conditioning. To stop would be to undermine our way of life. But the follower of the Tao knows the meaning of *enough*.

- If you were content with what you have, would you stop working? Or would you begin to work at that which is truly creative and transforming for the world?

I am content . . . with what I have.

163

Identifying with our true nature, we also understand that we are adequate for our death. (33)

Our survival instinct is important. It keeps us alert and aware. It generates compassion for the transient nature of all beings. But it is not the deepest truth. It strives for a lifetime and always fails. When we realize the futility of this, we allow our relationship with death to take its proper place.

- Relax and allow the flow of death and life to be. What's next after death? I don't know, but in the Tao there is always something next.

I can live . . . and die in peace.

164

The great Tao is like an ocean. It fills the universe and all things rely upon it. (34)

It's the old story of two fish swimming in the Pacific. One says to the other, "I don't think I believe in this thing called water. I mean, have you ever seen it?" The Tao is a paradox of vastness and hiddenness. We swim in it. We are made of it. Belief in it is incidental and only serves to keep us confused.

- Forget the concept called "belief." It is meaningless. What is, is. The Tao . . . is!

In the Tao . . . I swim.

165

The Tao gives us birth and never abandons us. (34)

We sometimes feel abandoned and alone, lost children in a fear-filled world. All the gods we have created have turned away from us, as all gods we create will do. But the Tao that was born as us still lives and grows as us. It cannot abandon itself. Neither can we abandon ourselves because we are the Tao, living as us.

- Don't abandon yourself. Your conditioned mind may turn away, but the essential you will never, ever turn away.

I was born . . . in the Tao.

166

The Tao does this marvelous work and needs no recognition. It nourishes us and sustains us yet does not claim to own us. (34)

How wonderful and freeing to know that the Tao wants nothing from us. It doesn't wait to pounce with jealous fury should we stray. It doesn't need our adoration or copious words of praise. We don't even have to call it "Tao." We don't have to call it anything at all.

- This path is not a burden or a test. It is simply a happy and free way to live. Enjoy it.

I am free . . . to be me.

167

The Tao has no need for glory, so it blends into the background and is hardly ever noticed. (34)

The Tao is truly humble. It hides inside of every atom of the cosmos and remains unnoticed. Being unnoticed, it is able to do its work completely. Perhaps we shouldn't even try to study it or "follow" it. Maybe we should just let it do its work in secret.

- Go ahead and see it. It doesn't mind. Just learn from its humility and don't preach.

I don't have to see . . . I can simply be.

168

The Tao is the true home to which we return, yet it wants no worship. No wonder we consider it great. (34)

When we walk through a lovely meadow where the birds are in full song and all the wildflowers are in spring bloom, we think, "How magnificent are the ways of the Tao. I should see the Tao in all the birds and in the flowers. I should give the Tao honor and thanks." The Tao whispers in a quiet voice in the desert breeze, "Don't think about me. Watch the birds and the flowers."

- You don't have to think good thoughts of the Tao. Simply enjoy.

Flowers . . . are flowers.

169

Our true greatness doesn't come from power or control. We just live our lives each moment as the greatness that we are. (34)

Taoist teachers through the ages were not movers and shakers. They were unnoticed. They stayed hidden, wanting only to live their lives in happy, peaceful simplicity. The few words they wrote come to us today because these words touch something deep within us, hidden beneath our conditioned thoughts. We are drawn to the Tao because it is us.

- Don't try to be great. Stay hidden.

Hidden . . . my life is as it should be.

170

Our practice looks beneath the passing thoughts that seem so real. (35)

Thoughts come and go. They are flickering images on the brain's wide-screen drama factory that captivate us and hold us fast. We come to believe that the drama is real, but these are biochemical impulses that flash at the speed of light. The brain is wonderful, but it has confused us with its constant conditioned thoughts.

- You are the viewer, not the film, the thinker, not the thoughts.

My thoughts . . . are not real.

171

Clinging to our thoughts brings pain. Letting them go brings joy and peace. (35)

If we mistake the dramatic film for reality, we suffer. Thoughts are actually very poor drama. Most of the thoughts we have today are identical to the ones we had yesterday, and the day before that. . . . Where are we going to find room in our mind for something new, something transformational? When we make room, transformation will happen!

- Empty your thoughts as you would empty a cup of stale coffee. Pour in something new.

I make room . . . for a new mind.

172

Lively music and good food may capture our attention, but speaking of this path is not exciting. (35)

Our daily thoughts are often a struggle with constant distraction. "I'm sleepy. What's happening over there? Let's get a snack." Staying present and doing our ordinary work is often not that thrilling. It's ordinary. But it's real. It is our path at this moment in our life and we find our happiness by continuing to walk along it.

- Dozens of distractions are pulling at your conditioned mind right at this moment. Recognize them. They are the opponent you must overcome.

I see how . . . I distract myself.

173

People would rather try to make things work, look for distractions, and listen to empty promises. (35)

Empty promises are some of the most powerful weapons of our conditioned mind. We bamboozle ourselves into believing that a new toy will bring us joy. We talk ourselves into zoning out in front of a screen, believing that "we are too tired." Media personalities promise us either doom or salvation. We actually mesmerize ourselves into believing that political meanness is good government.

- You live in the most distracted culture in human history. Stop it!

I will not . . . be distracted.

174

We turn to this path only when we have exhausted all other paths. (35)

Restlessness can be a sign that the usual distractions are not working. The games no longer amuse. The videos don't captivate. The toys break down. Finally, it dawns on us that we cannot distract ourselves anymore. Restlessness may be a positive indication. Perhaps we can't fix things by trying harder. Maybe there is another way waiting—a quiet, gentle, effortless way of attention and peace.

- This path is not one more distraction. It is a clear, honest experience of each precious moment.

I am tired . . . I will rest.

175

If we try to get rid of something, it will naturally remain. If we try to weaken a habit, it will naturally remain strong. If we try to push away our thoughts, they will naturally remain. (36)

Deeply embedded habits that have been reinforced by years of conditioned thinking have a tremendous staying power. The neural pathways in our brain have literally become addicted to a certain direction of flow by the creation of extra neuroreceptors that demand to be stimulated. Most attempts at change simply reinforce the same patterns by focusing attention on them. Without attention, they fade away.

- If you want to change a habit, be patient and imagine the brain pathways gradually reconfiguring themselves. Turn your attention to new ways of thinking.

I let old patterns . . . fade away.

176

If we try to get rid of our pain, we will suffer all the more. (36)

Of course we want our pain, physical or emotional, to end. Like our thoughts, however, when the pain is the focus of our attention it tends to increase in perceived intensity. It can't be ignored completely, but we might be able to place it in a larger container. We might be able to expand our awareness to include a greater perspective. The pain may remain, but the suffering diminishes.

- I'm sorry for whatever pain you are feeling. I hope you can breathe, relax a bit, and let your awareness grow to include the bigger cosmos.

I feel pain . . . but the suffering abates a bit.

177

On this path, gentleness and flexibility bring the results that force and rigidity fail to achieve. (36)

We sit at desks and feel our shoulders tighten as if it takes effort to depress the tiny computer keys. If we let our bodies relax and soften, we find that our mind also softens. A voice in our head says, “You have to get this work done today. You can’t relax!” Our Tao mind responds quietly, “Watch me.”

- Imagine you are a bamboo shoot, connected to all life around you. Notice how much more flexible and strong you feel.

I bend . . . but am not uprooted.

178

Our practice is one of effortless effort. It seems as if we do nothing, yet everything is done. (37)

Our hearts beat with tremendous energy yet without our conscious effort. Our breath rises and falls without our control. Nutrients flow, muscles grow and flex, nerves conduct the "chi" of life and we don't even notice that it's happening. Why in the world do we try so hard to make things happen?

- Marvelous things happen all by themselves. How much trust do you have that you will be okay?

I needn't control . . . anything.

179

If we stay on this path and resist the temptation to control, each thing will naturally evolve according to its individual nature. (37)

Our external world gets shaped by our internal world of fear and confusion. We try so hard to fix things and make a life that is safe. We push and shove, strive and stress to get and keep the things that promise security—but fail to deliver. Inner striving creates external chaos. Inner serenity and peace create external peace.

- Your future is your choice. The outer will mirror the inner. Choose.

I choose to remain . . . at peace.

180

When our conditioning attempts to stir things up, we return to the simple stillness. At this still point, our conditioned habits naturally fall away, leaving only peace. (37)

Our conditioned mind is filled with fear and strategies to allay that fear. Those strategies do not work. They only lead to more fear and more complicated strategies in a never-ending circle. Only when we put our thoughts in stillness and let our minds settle down will we find that we already have the peace we seek. All spiritual traditions tell us that peace is within us. We have never believed it.

- What if you actually did believe it? What if it were truly a simple choice?

I choose . . . stillness and peace.

181

Being good, while hoping for reward, has nothing to do with natural goodness. Natural goodness works effortlessly and benefits all. (38)

"Be a good boy," our mother always told us. Santa "knows if you've been bad or good, so be good for goodness sake," sings the awful holiday ditty. "God's watching you," intones despicable theology. We're left with a question, am I a good person? Or am I only good when I am doing good things as defined by other people?

- You are intrinsically good at the very core of your soul. Good actions come on their own.

I am . . . a good person.

182

Contrived goodness requires great effort and accomplishes very little. (38)

A great expenditure of energy in one direction always, just as in Newtonian physics, has an equal reaction in the opposite direction. Contrived goodness always meets resistance. But when we simply act naturally without conscious ego effort, true goodness occurs. Resistance has nothing against which to push.

- Stop trying to be good. Stop trying to do good. Let your life just happen. It will be good.

I don't have to . . . try so hard.

183

Compassion acts and seeks nothing. Justice acts and seeks specific results. (38)

Justice comes from the conditioned mind. It is perhaps a necessary element of society, but it is contrived to ensure obedience to the rules set by the leaders of that society. It basically attempts to protect property and life. Justice is always "judging" in an attempt to resolve conflict. Our inner compassion does not seek conflict but simply acts.

- Don't be so concerned with justice. It often simply means getting your own way.

Compassion . . . doesn't seek its own way.

184

Morality acts, then demands, and then forces correct behavior. (38)

If we have enough power, we can demand that others behave in a manner we find acceptable. Look at today's society to see what an exhausting way to live this "morality" really is. We can sometimes coerce behavior, but force will never, ever change or transform another person. Coerced behavior will eventually backfire on us.

- Let others believe and order their lives to please themselves. Then you can rest.

I cannot change . . . another person.

185

When we are separated from our true nature, we turn to rules of goodness. (38)

It begins with gold stars in kindergarten. We want children to learn proper social skills, but we forget that they need guidance, not reward and punishment. We would like children to "be good," but we forget that they are good. Our task is to show them their goodness and help them express it in appropriate ways.

- Did punishment ever make you "good"? I don't mean good behavior. I mean actually change you inside from "bad" to "good."

I can coerce behavior . . . not attitudes.

186

When we fail at being good, we make more detailed rules to govern our relationships. (38)

We are kind people. If we forget a thank-you note, we remain kind people and will usually remember. We sometimes act irritably, but we remain kind people and will usually behave graciously. We don't need to be subject to the "Kindness Cops." All we need to do is be ourselves.

- You are a kind person. Just pay attention to the present moment and trust yourself.

I am . . . kind.

187

When our relationships suffer, we insist on justice and fairness. Not finding justice or fairness, we all agree to pretend that empty rituals will suffice. (38)

Society is obsessed with rules for behavior—always the behavior of "other people." Those who are caught in this obsession forget that rules will lead to the appearance of goodness, never to the virtue itself. We end up spending a lot of time pretending. Things seem to be polite and courteous on the surface, but underneath we know that nothing has changed.

- Stop pretending. Look deep into what lies underneath our rules.

I want . . . what is real.

188

With this practice we find clarity. (39)

The incessant barrage of opinions and beliefs leaves us wondering just what is going on. Are things this way or that way? What should we do about it? The Tao holds no opinions or beliefs. It simply flows, and if we are watching, we can also simply see and flow. The way through the chaos and confusion will appear.

- Forget your opinions. Be still and watch until you see.

I watch . . . and wait . . . and see.

189

Our horizons become expansive. (39)

Our lives are confined by boxes of our own making. The walls of the boxes give us the illusion of security. We'd rather not think or see or act beyond the walls we make. A universe of limitless possibility waits for those who take even a small step outside the familiar ways of thinking.

- Your thoughts are the bars of your prison. What might wait on the other side?

I make my walls . . . I can unmake them.

190

Our daily life becomes tranquil. (39)

We tend to view a tranquil person as somehow deluded and perhaps lazy and self-centered. So many things need to be improved and fixed—how dare a person be content? Yet contentment is the very nature of a life lived in the Tao. Only from this place can effective action emerge.

- The world does not need your striving. It needs what will arise from your basic tranquility.

At peace . . . I serve best.

191

Our souls become inspired. (39)

The Tao is in the process of growing and sustaining the entire cosmos, seen and unseen. Here we are in the midst of it with all that cosmic energy flowing through us. Of course we live with creative passion. When we open to this energy, we will come alive. How could we not?

- Passionate living does not require your willpower. It simply requires an awareness of who you truly are.

I live . . . with passion.

192

Our relationships become filled with trust and honesty. (39)

The entire "self-help" section of the bookstore cannot supply enough wisdom to ensure that two egos get along. Ego relationships are through two conditioned minds. But when two souls meet outside the cluttered confines of the conditioned mind, they will discover their oneness with ease.

- Heal your mind, your relationships will follow.

My soul . . . to your soul.

193

Our society flourishes and everything around us becomes filled with creative life. (39)

Within the Tao, societies are built on mutual support. Outside of the Tao, they are built on "interest groups" at war with each other. Election time reveals our lack of creative conviction. Is there ever a candidate who says, "We must live more simply so that others may simply live?"

- Voting will not save society. A new understanding of humanity is the only hope. What will you do to help that come about?

Elections . . . or transformation?

194

Rather than clattering about trying to be noticed, we just roll along like common stones in the river. (39)

A person may not own a suit but enjoy being neat, clean, and healthy. A person may live in a cozy townhouse and have a refrigerator filled with healthy food. A person's bed may be warm and comfortable and hot water comes at their bidding from the magic pipes within the wall. We all have so very much, yet we crave attention and recognition. How could we want more?

- Why be noticed? Why want more? What are you doing?

Unnoticed . . . a common stone at peace within the river.

195

Following this path returns us to our root. It is a tender and gentle path. (40)

We emerge from the Tao and return to the Tao. T. S. Eliot knew that when we return we will know the place for the first time. When we feel like strangers in a strange land, it is good to keep this in mind. It's nice to remember that we are going home to an existence we will recognize at last as truly ours.

- Does this comfort you? Is it a bit frightening?

I'm going . . . home.

196

Everything in the cosmos depends on everything else. (40)

Independence is a myth. Although it usually feels like we are isolated and apart, we don't stand apart from it all, trying to somehow figure it all out. We are within the Whole and live as part of it, dependent on the functioning of the earth and all its gifts. If we accept that we are completely interdependent, we will stop our futile striving to be independent.

- Are you really self-sufficient? Or is that an illusion? List ten things upon which you depend.

I depend . . . on all that is.

197

Even our experience of life depends upon our death. (40)

We hear that "dark matter" makes up most of the matter in the universe—holds it all together, as a matter of fact. Something that can't be seen, measured, or understood somehow holds the whole thing together. And most of it is empty space, as are we. Perhaps our lives are held in place by our deaths.

- Life seems so solid, but it isn't. It needs the mystery of death to make it whole and real.

I am life . . . and death together.

198

The most helpful response to this path is to devote ourselves to it and practice it diligently. (41)

We wonder whether we have ever really been devoted, wholeheartedly, to something. Have we ever had a completely undivided mind? So often there is a tiny part of our conditioned mind that is holding back, sitting in judgment, and offering a commentary. We're trained to hedge our bets in the name of safety.

- Does holding back really keep you safe?

With all my heart . . . I devote myself.

199

But most people practice it only half-heartedly . . . (41)

If we try to follow the Tao with our conditioned mind, we will sometimes see clearly and sometimes be deluded. We may accomplish some things but will often exhaust ourselves by our own resistance—like driving with one foot on the gas and the other on the brake. We don't mean to resist, but it seems to happen unconsciously. We're not bad because of this, but it wastes a lot of energy.

- How much of the stress and fatigue in your life is self-imposed?

I take my foot . . . off the brake.

200

. . . and some people disregard it entirely, seeing it as absurd. (41)

Our conditioned mind insists that it is the only game in town. To quit the game, it insists, is foolishness and folly. Society will trample us underfoot. We laugh at the Tao and continue to turn the wheel in our rat cage. To actually value a spiritual path is somehow seen as wishful thinking or idealistic, even perhaps a sign of weakness. We never see how wonderful the power of the Tao might be.

- Disregard it if you want. It still remains the only reality. When you're ready, you'll see.

I laugh at it . . . but it remains.

201

The way to clarity will seem confusing. (41)

Confirmation bias works its insidious way on us. We look for opinions and interpret events in ways that will support what our conditioned minds have already decided. Our conditioning is terrified of confusion, of the necessity of reconciling complicated issues in ways that ultimately lead to deeper understanding. We would rather find easy answers, and plenty of people are ready to supply them.

- If you're not confused, you're not paying attention. Accept it as the way to clarity.

I welcome . . . confusion.

202

The way to progress will seem like going backward. (41)

When we are not so obsessed with "getting ahead" and "making progress," circling around and starting over will not be a problem. It will actually be the way to wisdom. The path will show us new perspectives and vistas the second time around. Perhaps the third time around will show us even more. Straight-line paths in life are rare and can be deceiving. Starting over is not a failure. It is just another step.

- Stop trying to get ahead. Simply look around and see what's happening.

I don't need . . . to get ahead.

203

The smoothest way will seem filled with obstacles. (41)

An obstacle may call forth creative problem-solving. It may cause us to think outside the box and come up with something entirely new. It may build mental muscle. Or it may simply say, "Take another route." In any case it is essential to our journey. Wise travelers welcome obstacles. They make the route interesting.

- What is, is. You might as well assume it is for your benefit.

Obstacles . . . make my way smooth.

204
The greatest power will lie in receptivity. (41)

We seldom know the names of those who have true power. They aren't those who can bomb cities from afar or make the world into their own toxic sandbox. The truly powerful never look for fame or have their name upon a building. They do not have followers or Facebook likes. They are content to be unknown and available to the Tao in whatever form it takes.

- Are you available? Really? To anything?

I am . . . available and receptive.

205

True innocence will appear shameful. (41)

If we don't strive for more, we will be called lazy. If we refuse to fight and kill, we will be called cowards. If we are tenderhearted, we will be called soft. If we desire a simple and just life for all people, we will be called commie-socialists. If we choose to love the wrong person, we will be called immoral.

- What are you willing to be called?

I don't care . . . what I am called.

206

The greatest resources will appear inadequate. (41)

Enough is enough, they say. How much is that? Where do I get it? How do I keep it? Our conditioned mind does not know. The Tao requires a simple willingness to know the meaning of "enough." If we don't know what enough is, we will never have it. Enough looks different depending on whether we see with conditioned mind or with Tao mind. Strangely, most rich people do not believe they have enough yet.

- With what eyes do you judge "enough"?

I know . . . enough.

207

Genuine goodness will appear suspect. (41)

We will be called naive and unrealistic. We will be seen as weak and gullible. Our compassion will be dismissed as sentimental. Our convictions will be called snobbery. We will not be feted, paraded, or sainted. Goodness flowing naturally from the Tao will be all we have. Why would we want more?

- You can be admired . . . or truly good. Your choice.

I choose . . . true goodness.

208

The truly solid and dependable will seem uncertain. (41)

No one likes uncertainty. We don't know what the Tao will do or which way it will flow from one moment to the next. We have to trust that it knows where it is going and that we are along for the ride. We steer according to the path the moment presents. We adjust course at a moment's notice. This is true security.

- Can you not know—not have the faintest idea—and still trust?

I trust . . . myself in the moment.

209
The wisest person will always be learning. (41)

Lao-tzu was called a "fool" for rejecting fame and fortune in favor of a simple and unknown life. What society calls wisdom is actually frightening. People that culture admires have a facade of wisdom, but inside they are afraid and insecure, unwilling to admit ignorance and learn something new. Following the Tao, we want to laugh and dance and make a fool out of ourselves, to make people wonder about us.

- Don't try to be wise. Be willing to be foolish. It's more fun and more Tao-like.

I am . . . a happy fool.

210

This path, silent and without form, is the way to all beauty and joy. (41)

"Look at me!" cries artificial beauty. Artificial happiness is loud and calls attention to itself. "Look how happy I am!" The beauty of the Tao is unnoticed in the wrinkled smile of the aged; the textured, weathered wood of a barn; and the flower blooming in a hidden place no one will ever see.

- Look around and find something small, unnoticed, ordinary. Look closely and see the depth of true beauty.

Beauty lies . . . in hidden places.

211

Every atom of the cosmos contains the yin and yang together. Yin and yang together produce the energy of creation and give rise to all things. (42)

Some Mystery at the heart of things divided itself in two and, *bang!* The universe began. The yin and yang remain essential, and nothing exists without their dance. It is true within the subatomic particles and also true within our lives. Carl Sagan said, "We are star stuff, standing up and looking back at the stars." We are the true extraterrestrial beings. We came from the stars!

- Can you feel this constant flowing dance?

I am . . . the stuff of stars.

212

We feel this harmonious process in the rising and falling of our breath. (42)

The still point where one breath ends and the next begins is a place of harmony. Things are always going round and round or up and down. We can become pretty disoriented if we live on the edge of this process. If we live near the center, we can see without so much confusion. The outer world is chaotic, but there is a way to see all that and still have an essential stillness.

- Are you living near the center?

My life . . . is at the center.

213

It seems natural to seek gain and avoid loss, but on this path these distinctions are not helpful. There is no gain without loss. There is no fullness without deprivation. (42)

There is a minimalist flavor to Taoist thought that is contrary to cultural norms. Acquisition is not considered helpful; indeed, it tends to separate one more and more from the Tao. The more one acquires, the less space one has for simple pleasures and authentic joy. Eventually the wheel must turn and it is best to cooperate with its turning.

- How much space do you have in your life right now? Physical and emotional? (They are closely connected.)

I have space . . . for life and joy.

214

So we remain at the center and trust events instead of forcing them. This is the heart of all spiritual paths. (42)

Without stillness there can be no connection. We must be able to sit quietly and alone for a whole morning or afternoon without reading, viewing, or talking. If we can't do this, no amount of screen time will ever assuage our loneliness.

- Can you? Can you spend a whole morning in a quiet place? Why not? How can you cultivate that kind of stillness?

I come . . . to the quiet.

215

The most fluid and yielding substance will flow past the most rigid with the speed of a racehorse. (43)

A violent storm rages through a nearby park. Ancient oak trees stand rigid against the wind and their branches are found strewn about the park the next morning. Some giants are even uprooted entirely. There is a bamboo grove along the stream in this same park. After the storm we find only a few leaves on the ground.

- How strong are you? Can you bend in the storm?

Soft . . . supple . . . strong.

216

That which does not hold a particular form can enter even that which seems impenetrable. (43)

Each moment is an empty space, available to the Tao. But we want to fill it up and hold it in place so we don't have to be anxious about our safety. Emptiness is unsettling, but so necessary. Today we can sit here and read and let the words come into an empty space, rest in our mind, then flow out, and the space is empty yet again. The words come and go.

- Can you empty your mind each time you empty your lungs? This makes room for fresh thoughts along with the fresh air.

Empty . . . fill . . . empty . . . fill.

217

This is why we practice wu wei. We act without ado. We teach without arguments. (43)

One foot on the gas, the other on the brake all day every day. We are always getting in our own way. We must do this. We must explain this clearly. We must succeed. We must be liked and respected. What if we stopped listening to these idiotic voices and just did things: walked, read, painted, wrote, worked, rested, ate, washed, et cetera?

- Let go of must. Let go of should. Let go and just *do.*

I do . . . without resistance.

218

This is the way to true happiness. But, because people prefer distractions, it is not a popular way. (43)

We might sit at our desk with only the sounds of a nearby fan in our ears. The distractions are, however, running rampant in our minds. Voices are telling us what we should be doing, what we should fear, what we should have for lunch, and how we're somehow not quite enough. Have we seen the news? Have we checked email? Distraction is inevitable.

- Remember: where you put your attention determines the quality of your life.

Quiet . . . attentive . . . happy.

219

Is fame worth the sacrifice of our true nature? (44)

We learn to judge ourselves by checking to see what others think of us. Why in the world is what others think any of our business? Will I die if you don't like what I write? ("Well," says the voice, "if they don't like what you write, you won't get paid and you'll end up starving under a freeway overpass.") Nonsense! Pleasing others never really pleases anyone. No one needs another "like" on social media.

- You're going to die no matter what you do. Do what pleases you.

I please . . . myself.

220

Which causes more suffering—accumulating things or letting them go? (44)

The moment we have it, we might lose it. So we must keep it safe, find a place to store it, clean it, worry about it, and insure it. Were we to lose it, all that fuss would disappear. What's the fuss about anyway? To paraphrase the words from Kris Kristofferson's song "Me and Bobby McGee": freedom is another way of saying there's nothing left to lose.

- How free do you really want to be?

Laying it down . . . I am free.

221

Looking outside ourselves for approval and security, we find only suffering. (44)

There is nothing outside of us that we can count on controlling. It is changing every moment and the part of us that counts on things staying stable will always be afraid. Today's unsocial media creates a false sense of worthiness or unworthiness based on likes and dislikes. It is difficult to develop any true sense of self in such a world. We must have ways of disengaging from the outside world on a regular basis, just to keep our perspective clear.

- Don't give up your self-sovereignty for any reason.

Approval or disapproval . . . I am the same.

222

Understanding that we are capable for our lives, we stop exhausting ourselves and begin enjoying ourselves. (44)

We want companionship. We want support. We want affirmation. We want all the benefits of popularity and wealth. In the end, though, all we have is ourselves. That will have to be enough. Remember the old spiritual: "You got to walk that lonesome valley. You got to walk it by yourself. Nobody else can walk it for you. You got to walk it by yourself."

- You got to walk it by yourself. You can do it.

I can walk . . . it by myself.

223

True perfection does not exhaust itself trying to appear perfect. (45)

Seeking perfection is a waste of time. We're already perfect. We're perfectly well, perfectly sick, or perfectly somewhere in between. Whatever we are in a given moment, we are perfectly that. We can work to improve our life and the lives of others, but working for perfection is a way to perpetual misery. Each moment along the path is perfectly what it is.

- What is . . . is! That's the way it is! What are you going to do now?

I work with . . . what is.

224

True abundance does not waste itself in showy displays. (45)

Our conditioned mind creates a stage show of our life and presents it to itself, playing both actor and audience. Life is not a stage show! It is our life and does not need an audience, internal or external. Our loved ones are not our audience. We do not have to put on a show for them. They don't need a show. They need our attention, compassion, and love.

- Stop acting. Stop cheering or booing yourself. Just live and enjoy.

My life is not . . . a show.

225

The most helpful words will appear hesitant. (45)

People rant and rave with the appearance of great wisdom and confidence, but their words are empty. The more forceful the words, the more we can be sure that we are being manipulated and used. Treat the great orators with a degree of mistrust and turn instead to the friend who says, "I'm not sure, but I want to help. How can I help?"

- Who will sit quietly with you and tell you the difficult truths? Trust this person.

I trust . . . a quiet presence.

226

When we see clearly, we act with tranquility, and exactly what is needed is done. (45)

We can build castles in the air made from the vapor of our desires, but they are not real and will disappear in an instant. If we build our lives from the reality of the present moment, we will have a certain calmness that comes from knowing we are doing what is actually needed. Dreams are helpful when they serve as a direction for our work. The work itself emerges from that which is in front of us in the moment.

- Look around at what there is to do today. Don't complain that it isn't enough. It is enough. What can you make of it?

I do . . . what is needed.

227

When we practice this path, our energy is focused on useful, helpful projects. (46)

Nothing is more satisfying than the feeling that we have somehow contributed to something good and true and helpful. As we align with the flow of the Tao, the projects that are in accordance with this impulse appear as if by magic. We are invited to do them as expressions of our true nature. Such work is often difficult to discover in a chaotic world.

- What do you do that is truly good and helpful? What stops you?

I want . . . to create good.

228

When we depart from this path, fear contaminates our energy and we become concerned with self-protection. (46)

Have you noticed that the bulk of our economy is focused on the military, weapons, social media, sports, and trivial things? We are a terrified society and therefore are willing to be distracted by toys and games while allowing weapons to proliferate. We argue that it is necessary. No one dares to disagree.

- What are you doing?

I want to make . . . something useful.

229

Our greatest suffering comes from not knowing who we are or where we belong. (46)

That nagging feeling that we are clueless as to where we come from and where we are going cannot be repressed forever. We can divert and distract ourselves for only so long. Eventually we must face the fundamental questions of our existence. Who am I? What am I doing here? These questions do have answers, but our conditioned mind tends to avoid them.

- Who are you? What are you doing here?

I can face . . . the questions.

230

Our greatest unhappiness comes from always wanting something more, something else. (46)

We might say that we are content and happy, until we look closely at the way our minds churn throughout the day, telling us all the things we need. While waiting for our car to be serviced, we suffer thinking of all the things we should be doing. We can be frustrated that they are taking so long. Or we can take the opportunity to sit still and let our attention rest on something beautifully ordinary around us while our thoughts settle down.

- Which choice do you make? Why?

I choose . . . contentment.

231

To be content with each breath is to be eternally content. This is our practice. (46)

Contentment isn't waiting for us down the road a bit. We don't have to get the ducks in a row (a futile task anyway). We don't have to feel better or solve all our problems. The choice is offered every single moment of every single day. Contentment is available here and now. It isn't complicated. It isn't really difficult. It is always just a choice of where to place our attention.

- Again, make a choice. Now.

Again I choose . . . contentment.

232

It is not necessary to travel to understand the world. (47)

It's not about taking a trip. It is about where our minds wander in their attempts to understand. We wander in religions, philosophies, politics, relationships, and esoteric musings. We dream that another home, job, or relationship might improve our life. What is necessary is to simply be at home, completely at home, right where we are, right now.

- Where are you? What time is it?

I am here . . . the time is now.

233

It is not necessary to look out the window to see into ourselves. The more we look outside ourselves for knowledge, the less we know about anything. We do not wander about, yet still we gain knowledge. We do not look about, yet still we gain understanding. (47)

In the world of the Internet, do we actually understand any of the stuff we know? We know the Andromeda galaxy is more than two million light-years away from us, but we don't understand the immensity and emptiness that lie in between. We know how to click an online shopping cart, but we don't understand the need to do so. We know the sports scores, but we don't know why they are important.

- What, among all the things you "know," do you really understand?

I want . . . to understand.

234

We do not strive, yet still we accomplish everything. (47)

Striving has an edge about it. A need to get somewhere or do something seems to constantly drive us. On the other hand, working with enthusiasm and energy can have a relaxed flow, a pleasure in simply being where we are. It doesn't need an edge. It is a work of pleasure. If we pay attention, we can tell the difference.

- Which way does your daily work unfold?

I work . . . with flow and ease.

235

Seeking knowledge, we add new facts each day. Seeking the Tao, we drop assumptions each day. Each day we assume less and less, until we assume nothing. There is nothing left to do and nothing left undone. (48)

Some of us have studied theology in an effort to understand God. This assumed that God was just a field of inquiry. We had our own esoteric terms that made us seem quite erudite, but we were merely silly geese, honking in the wilderness. The Tao is not a subject of study; it is the air in our lungs and the joy in our hearts. When we stopped studying and talking endlessly about God—we were suddenly with God.

- Don't study Taoism. That is dry dust. Live the Tao.

I assume . . . nothing.

236

Allowing things to come and go according to their nature, we gain everything. Trying to control everything, we gain nothing. (48)

We persist in thinking that, if we work harder, we will do a better job. We believe that the more control we exert, the better the outcome will be. But guiding is more effective than interfering and cooperating is more effective than controlling. Understanding how a task actually wants to be done is the key to doing that task.

- Are you helping people and situations? Or are you trying to force them to be what you want them to be?

I allow . . . I accomplish.

237

We hold no fixed opinions. Our hearts are therefore open to the hearts of all. (49)

Sometimes our conversations remind me of dogs nosing each other's behinds. We sniff out each other's stances on sports, politics, and religion. Then we use the old "And what do you do?" to establish the economic pecking order. Then we wonder why the world is filled with mistrust and violence. There is a different way of relating that begins with the assumption that we are all part of the same life and that we all, deep down, want the same things.

- How many of your conversations each day have a goal apart from positioning yourself?

My heart is open . . . to all.

238

We extend kindness to the kind and unkind alike. Therefore, kindness becomes our very nature. (49)

Kindness is not a strategy for getting ahead in life. It is not a technique to get results. It is not a squishy sentiment for those who need to be liked. It is our very nature and we are happiest when we allow it to flow regardless of the situation, when we begin with kindness rather than waiting for the other person to be kind.

- What situations are most difficult for you to be kind in?

Kindness is . . . my nature.

239

We extend trust to the trustworthy and untrustworthy alike. Therefore, trust becomes our very nature. (49)

We don't have to trust that everything will work out the way we want. We don't have to trust that people will behave the way we want them to. We can trust that events and people will be exactly what and who they are, and we can accept and understand them. Knowing this, we are able to trust our own nature and our responses to situations and people.

- Trust yourself and your responses. Let people and events be themselves.

I trust . . . my own responses.

240

We don't contend with people by seeking to gain advantage. People around us lose their edge and we become loving friends to the whole world. (49)

Our inner business manager insists that we seek our own advantage in every transaction. "This," he says, "is how the system works." Advantage over whom, we wonder? Must someone lose in order that we might win and be safe? This requires us to be on constant guard and always somewhat afraid. Is that the life we want?

- Do you seek your own advantage? Is your life a win or lose game?

No one needs to lose . . . for me to win.

241

Life and death are inseparable. One is form, and the other is formless. Each gives way to the other. (50)

The sun burns itself up. Each day it transforms its material elements into heat and light, thus giving us warmth and life. Each day we consume the elements of our life, giving ourselves up to bring creative compassion and love into being. Living and dying are the same thing.

- We may as well give off warmth and light while we are using ourselves up.

I give myself up . . . and live in love.

242

Some people concentrate on life and ignore death. (50)

A death-denying culture forgets its own natural limits. If we forget death, we never stop to think about the consequences of our actions. We take loved ones for granted and forget to love and cherish them. We use up the earth's resources, stockpile trinkets, and seek to win, succeed, and grow forever.

- What essential truth does death teach you?

Death defines . . . my life.

243
Some people obsess over death and ignore life. (50)

Aging either brings new horizons of freedom or the prison bars of fear. Unless there is a reawakening to life, people begin to shut down and take refuge in the offices of doctors and specialists. One test follows another and procedures keep death at bay. But it remains just outside the door. Life becomes smaller and smaller.

- Once again, as always, the choice of freedom or captivity is yours.

I choose . . . life.

244

Some people ignore both life and death and just pass on through. (50)

Either ignoring death or obsessing over it will bring suffering. But ignoring both death and life is the worst suffering of all. This is often the choice in a society that offers diversions, distractions, and illusions at every turn. No need to concern ourselves, just click, swipe, like, dislike, tweet, and post until the end.

- The choice of embracing both death and life is seldom made. Can you make it?

I choose . . . life . . . and death.

245

Life and death have become the same; therefore, even death cannot disturb us. (50)

"Don't you realize that I could kill you without batting an eye?" the soldier shouted. To which the master calmly responded, "Don't you realize that I could die without batting an eye?" At this the soldier threw himself at the master's feet and became his disciple. Being ready for either life or death at each instant is the greatest of powers.

- Are you ready? Clear, grateful, and with eyes wide open?

Without . . . batting an eye.

246

The Tao expresses itself in each and every being. (51)

It's all the Tao. Everywhere we look we are seeing the Tao. The beetle and the dung it eats are the Tao. The supernova in the sky and the sand on the beach are the Tao. The air and the water are the Tao. The woman who annoys us in the grocery line is the Tao. The beautiful and the ugly are the Tao. Our lover and our enemy are the Tao. You are the Tao and I am the Tao.

- Remember that whatever you see, whatever you touch, is holy. Where you are standing now is holy ground. It's all holy ground.

This is . . . holy ground.

247

Each and every being honors the Tao and delights in its presence, not because they are commanded but because it is their nature. (51)

The Tao has no holy books. It issues no commandments. It wants no rituals, priests, or temples. These things are of limited use. They are products of the conditioned mind's attempt to put things in boxes and feel the illusion of control. The Tao wants only the joy of living, free and effortless in our hearts.

- Don't mistake your desires for control and safety for the wishes of the Tao.

I honor the Tao . . . with my joy.

248

The Tao sustains us, develops us, teaches us, shelters us, matures us, and returns us to our origin. (51)

The presence and guidance of the Tao is not a narrow set of rules to follow or a tightrope to walk in constant danger of falling. It is a gracious presence that fills our inmost being. Nothing can separate us from it. We can't avoid it no matter how we try. We are eternally safe within it.

- Relax! You are in the Tao right now. You are safe.

I am safe . . . within the Tao.

249

The Tao gives us life but does not claim to own us. (51)

You do not belong to the Tao like a possession. How can the Tao own something when everything is the Tao? The Tao is not a god, standing outside of creation and making possessive and jealous noises, doling out reward and punishment. It needs nothing from us, so we are free to live.

- You have ultimate freedom, even to create destruction. But, knowing what you know, why in the world would you want to?

I am free . . . to live.

250

The Tao is our true guide but does not control us. Its presence is deep within the heart of every being. (51)

It might seem easier if the Tao would issue orders. "Do this! Don't do that!" We seem to be left to find our way through our fear and confusion. But when we stop and come to a silent, still point within, we do find subtle guidance. We are not alone and adrift, though it sometimes feels as if we are.

- No matter how adrift and confused you feel, there is a place of guidance. It is subtle and easily missed amid the chaos of our world. But trust me. It is there.

I am not . . . alone.

251

The origin of all that is can naturally be called "mother of all." (52)

So many of our cultural images of the Divine are masculine. This is only half the truth. Lao-tzu focuses on the Divine feminine and sees the cosmos as a "child of the mother" rather than a separate creation. Either image is simply a metaphor, but the mother image contains a sense of nurture that we often miss.

- You are a child of the cosmos, not an interloper. You belong.

I am . . . nature's child.

252

If we let our thoughts become still and our needs become few, we will live in peace. (52)

Our mind actually wants to quiet down. It has been trained to process constant stimulation, but it really prefers the stillness. If we are patient and allow our thoughts to drift away without adding stimulation, we will discover a surprising tranquility waiting. The mind will relax. It honestly wants to be quiet.

- Don't try to meditate. Just don't add anything to your mind for a period of time. See what happens.

I can find . . . stillness.

253

If we follow our thoughts and chase after distractions, we will live in chaos. (52)

A man once wrote a very good book on meditation. He wanted to title it "My Mind Is an Asshole," but his editor wouldn't allow it. It's an accurate title, though. What else would you call that endless harping voice? (The title ended up being *10% Happier: How I Tamed the Voice in My Head* by Dan Harris.)

- That voice is not your friend. Learn to ignore it.

I don't listen . . . to harping voices.

254

Noticing small and ordinary things is enlightenment. (52)

It is nothing special, no great visions, no grandiose plans to change the world, no lofty goals to make us strain and strive to satisfy our egos. It is simply tasting the hot coffee in the presence of a good friend. It is listening to jazz when no one is around and becoming lost in the music. Or it might be writing a poem no one will ever read. It is happiness in the present moment.

- When the ordinary moment becomes your focus, your life will transform. I promise.

I notice . . . ordinary things.

255

Enlightenment is our natural state. Sitting in meditation, we see our hidden suffering, accept it, lay it down, and return to peace. (52)

There is always enough wisdom, enough courage, enough insight, and enough willingness to take the next step in our lives. It is nothing big or momentous. It is simply seeing clearly what the next small step might be, then taking it. It may be closing this book and making lunch. It's that simple.

- What's next for you?

I simply do . . . whatever's next.

256

It takes just a tiny bit of willingness to follow this path, but many things distract us. (53)

We would rather do an online crossword puzzle than grapple with the reality of our lives. It is only a click away. Maybe we could check our email and get another cup of coffee. We live in a culture that fails to practice attention, don't we? The good news is that only a tiny bit of willingness can turn our attention back to our true path.

- Where does your attention want to go right now? Can you turn it to the sights, sounds, and aromas of the present moment?

I am . . . willing.

257

This path is broad and steady, but we are conditioned to follow our thoughts down countless sidetracks. (53)

It really is our thoughts that lead us astray. A hundred distractions are available in every moment, but it is our mind that makes the choice. That choice is so often made out of unconscious habit rather than awareness. Beautiful, positive, and helpful choices are available if we take a moment to consider them.

- The quality of your life right now depends on where you choose to place your attention.

I choose . . . to be here, now.

258

Those who can afford distractions gather them by the carload, while the basic needs of most go unmet. (53)

The world is interdependent. Everything is connected. Feeling guilty and punishing ourselves will only cause us to avoid seeing where we can do our part to spread compassion. Instead, we can let our awareness gently skew our actions toward simplicity. This will begin to change the world because the world is us.

- Don't argue. Don't justify. Just live the life you know is right.

I am . . . connected to the whole world.

259

The accumulation of luxuries is a futile attempt to find happiness by taking that which is not freely given. (53)

The simple life is not simple, is it? Our habits are so ingrained and seem so natural that we seldom notice that our life flies by, unnoticed, while we are lost amid the bright colors and the cacophony of sounds and the myriad things to buy. Notice that much of this accumulation is actually "taking" that which is not freely given by nature.

- Make one day each week a "no-buy" day. (Maybe two days each week?)

I am not . . . my toys.

260

If we establish ourselves on this path, we will not be shaken by events. (54)

We will not be immune to the external events that form a sometimes chaotic backdrop to our lives. We can, however, find a stability underneath the events that keeps us from being blown over. It's useless to try to anticipate events to find that stability. The stability comes from our everyday, moment-by-moment attention to our lives.

- Don't worry. Worry is not preparation. Just pay attention. You'll do fine.

I am standing . . . on a solid place.

261

If we take this path into our hearts, our children and their children will benefit. (54)

We don't have to leave a large estate. We don't have to do great things according to economic standards. We don't have to be wise in everything we say. But we can be real. We can be close to nature. We can have a quiet spirit. People will remember this and think of us when we've passed. . . . "They had peace and joy."

- What are you leaving behind for loved ones to remember?

I want to leave memories . . . of a quiet, loving spirit.

262

This path brings our communities a lasting legacy and our countries true prosperity. (54)

In the chaos of today's world, it is easy to feel that we are people without a country. We tend to look outside ourselves and blame our culture for not being more Tao-like. We must turn around and look within ourselves and ask again about the legacy we are leaving and the kind of country we are cultivating in our hearts.

- It's not about the country. It's about you.

I want to be . . . what I want my country to be.

263

We practice awareness in each and every moment. We see ourselves in every person we meet. The whole world becomes our family, our community, our country. (54)

We don't have to make our family, our community, or our country behave. We don't have to force our Taoist ideas upon them. We simply have to see ourselves clearly and do what is the next thing for us to do. No forcing. No strain. Just being still and attentive and letting our doing emerge from that.

- You don't have to change a thing "out there." Just see clearly.

The world . . . is my home.

264

How do we make this discovery? By sitting still and looking within. (54)

It all boils down to us. There is no shortcut waiting out there for us to find. We must find enough stillness to finally see this truth. It's all inside. And it's not that hard. Stillness is always waiting and can be felt with just a moment's shifting of attention. It's where Jesus said the realm of heaven truly lives and it is the only thing that truly satisfies.

- Please find consistent ways of coming to a still and quiet place—however it works for you.

What I am seeking . . . is already inside of me.

265

Embracing this path, we are like newborn children. Our body is soft and flexible, yet strong. (55)

Children must be taught tension. It is not a natural quality. First stiffness and rigidity are patterned into their minds. Then they find their way to the muscles in the chest and face. This tension is not natural and can be released with practice. Think of returning once again to the mind and body of a child.

- First, notice how tense you are. Then relax your muscles one group at a time. Start by simply letting your shoulders drop into a restful position.

I release . . . my tension, mind and body.

266

We are in harmony with all creatures, bringing harm to none. (55)

The wilderness around us is, for most, an unknown and vaguely threatening environment. But we have a natural intelligence that, if cultivated, will let us enjoy nature in all its forms while remaining aware and safe. Only actual danger alerts us, not our conditioned fears. We don't have to pave paradise in order to be safe.

- Most of your fears are imaginary and can be dropped. Now the very few actual dangers can be dealt with.

I don't fear . . . my natural world.

267

Our vital passion is not limited to sexual intercourse but empowers all of life. (55)

Think of the creative energy and potential that are wasted in our sex-obsessed culture. What magnificent solutions to our problems have been dissipated in fantasy? What satisfying activities have we missed by squandering our power and potential? Sexual energy is simply energy and can be used in many creative ways for good.

- Sex is fine. But can we bring that same passion to other spheres of life?

My creative energy . . . is focused and powerful.

268

Our harmony and focus allow us to work all day at a single task and not grow tired. (55)

There is a vast difference between natural fatigue and the exhaustion that comes from useless tension and resistance. Thoughts about hard work can bring resistance and unnecessary fatigue. This is entirely different from the actual work itself. In that difference lies the distinction between honest fatigue and conditioned exhaustion.

- Stop thinking about it. Do it, or not. (Apologies to Yoda.)

I work . . . without exhaustion.

269

This harmony is experienced only in the present moment. It is in the present moment that we see the way ahead. (55)

Eternity is not the endless extent of time. It is the Tao before it gave birth to space and time. It is what surrounds us every moment. It is called "the present moment." It can't be grasped or explained, but it is, indeed, all there ever is. When we are there, we don't know it, because "we" disappear.

- Let it go. Shake time off your shoulders. Disappear into this moment.

I exist . . . only here and now.

270

Everything in life becomes a blessing. Forcing events to be other than what they are only brings misery. (55)

We can't make what "is not" into what we want without seeing clearly what it "is" in the first place. Once we see what actually "is," we might be able to see the next step we are to take. But trying to deny what is, or forcing it to change to suit our whims, will only make us miserable.

- You are free to take action, by all means. But first know, deep down, what you are dealing with.

I deal first . . . with what is.

271

The more we understand this path, the less we need to convince others. The more we need to convince others, the less we really understand. (56)

We think that if we could just explain it better, or perhaps yell louder, we could finally convince them of the rightness of our opinions. But this path does not need that from us. There is no need to be evangelists for a Taoist view. We have enough to do to keep our attention focused on our own footsteps.

- If you begin to argue this path, stop. That is not the way.

I don't need . . . to argue.

272

So we become silent and stop looking about for approval. (56)

The wonders of the cosmos are meant to be attended, absorbed, delighted in, revered, and appreciated. We don't have to get others to see things as we do. It's best to keep our mouth shut and simply smile and point. We don't have to be responsible for what other people see, but we are responsible for what we see. What we see makes all the difference.

- You love to share with others; that's natural. But do it silently.

Look . . . be quiet.

273

We cease taking offense at the opinions of others. (56)

If a person speaks from ignorance, what is that to us? Should we argue them into the truth? That always works so well, doesn't it? Most of China at the time of Lao-tzu considered him to be a crazy, good-for-nothing, lazy bum. Yet he never argued or defended himself. He simply lived according to his soul.

- You know, deep inside, the truth of your life. Remember it.

I know . . . who and what I am.

274

We no longer complicate our thinking or our lives. (56)

Some thoughts spring from the clear pool at the center of our Tao mind. These thoughts bring clarity and peace. Most thoughts emerge from the muddy waters of the conditioned mind: fear, envy, desires, opinions, and judgments. These bring confusion and suffering. The most important decision facing us is which of these to follow.

- Which thoughts are you letting direct your day?

I choose . . . my Tao mind.

275

We do not seek the spotlight but instead become a simple part of all that is. (56)

Sometimes we crave the notice of other people simply because it feels good to be acknowledged for good work. This feels natural and we wonder why the Tao cautions us in this area. It does seem a small thing to want acknowledgment, but to consciously seek that acknowledgment causes a fissure to form between our natural life and our conditioned work. It can be a small fissure, but a fissure nonetheless.

- What do you do for yourself alone?

I am a simple . . . part of all that is.

276

We can be loved or shunned, make a profit or suffer a loss, be honored or disgraced and never lose the treasure of our being. (56)

The part of us that wants to be liked, make more money, and become famous is not the part that we want to nurture. That part is terrified of not succeeding and would never let us rest if we tried to please it. We need to befriend the part of us that accepts with gratitude everything that happens. This one is our true friend.

- Make friends with the one inside you who knows, accepts, and delights. They are always there.

I am happy . . . with it all.

277

To guide a country, we use administrative skills. To gain joy in living, we let life live itself. (57)

"Administering" our lives implies setting goals, having purposes, and measuring their accomplishment. It seems wise but has many downsides. Goals and purposes tend to blind us to the unexpected and creative possibilities we hadn't dreamed of. A well-lived life is not a series of checked-off goals.

- Think of general intentions instead of concrete goals. Be open to unexpected guidance.

I intend . . . to be surprised.

278

The harder we try, the more our efforts fail. (57)

It seems counterintuitive, doesn't it? But notice how the muscles tighten, the thoughts become less expansive, the options narrow, and the desire to force square pegs into round holes increases. Of course we expend energy and take vigorous action when appropriate, but this is quite different from "trying too hard." It takes patience and skill to learn the distinction.

- Stop. Let your facial muscles relax, your shoulders drop, and your thoughts loosen up.

I relax my body . . . I work with ease.

279

The more we arm ourselves, the more chaos we experience. (57)

We create our personal and national defenses in response to our perception of threat. But the filters of fear distort our vision and cause us to see threats at every turn, in every situation, and across every ocean. So we increase our personal and national weaponry and our world becomes more and more dangerous. Our vision is clouded in fear and needs to become clear once again.

- Where does your safety actually lie? What will help you live or die in peace?

My safety does not lie . . . in my armored life.

280

The more schemes we devise, the less predictable are the results. (57)

Everyone is looking for an edge, an advantage, or a way up the ladder where they hope some room remains at the top. We get in each other's way and step on each other's toes. What would happen if we stayed off the ladder altogether? What's at the top that we don't have already available in simple things around us?

- Stay off the ladder. There's nothing up there.

I no longer . . . climb ladders.

281

The more rules we impose, the more we become rule breakers. (57)

If we have enough power, we may be able to impose our will on other people and force them to behave as we wish. But we must be vigilant. Underneath they will grow resentment, disdain, and ultimately rebellion. If you want your ducks to stay in place, give them a large lake in which to swim.

- No one wants to be controlled. Is there another option?

I live without rules . . . yet behave with love.

282

We stop trying to change ourselves and find that we naturally change. (57)

If we let our souls direct our actions, our actions slowly become exactly what we had hoped to accomplish with all our resolutions and goals. The internal resistance disappears because the actions and intentions arise from the same quiet place within us. The person we have always hoped to become is waiting for us to wake up and see them.

- If you want to change, you will. Watch and see.

I naturally become . . . the person I want to be.

283

We stop trying to be good and find that goodness is our nature. (57)

Natural goodness is there from the beginning. But we quickly learn to see ourselves as separate and at risk. Fear then contaminates our responses and we must develop wisdom and learn ways to connect with and express that goodness in social situations. This is not all bad, but it is not the same as goodness itself.

- You may not know yourself to be good, but you are. Let your actions reflect that.

I am . . . good.

284

We stop trying to get our own way and begin to enjoy our life. (57)

A bumper sticker tells us "Freedom Isn't Free," but it really is. True freedom is an inside thing. It is a choice we make about what guides our life. We can make that choice at any time. We can choose freedom from the nattering voices inside our head. We can choose freedom from the external expectations that burden our lives. That would be true freedom.

- Freedom from those voices is the choice you have before you in every moment. That work is true "freedom fighting."

I choose . . . freedom.

285

This path is unobtrusive, allowing the simple purity of those who follow it to emerge. If it were a path of interference and control, those who tried to follow it would soon turn aside. (58)

The Tao has no need to polish us, improve us, or fix us. It simply extends itself in front of our feet and invites us to walk along it. If we want to grow, learn, and strengthen ourselves because of an internal urge from within our own souls, we are welcome to do that. The Tao will support us. If we don't have that internal urge, that is fine with the Tao as well.

- If there was nothing you had to do and no one you had to be, what would you do? Who would you be?

I am free . . . to follow my soul.

286

What we call good fortune and bad fortune are mixed together in all events. If we try to have one without the other, we will become completely confused. (58)

When we try to ensure that only the "good" things happen, we ignore the natural flow of life and put a kink in the energy systems around us. We often end up harming ourselves and others by forcing things to go our way, ignoring hidden consequences. Besides, does that approach ever really work for us?

- It is fine to take prudent steps to benefit yourself and others. Just take care that you don't start thinking "good for me" is the greatest good.

I accept . . . the ups and downs without complaint.

287

One who follows this path will have firm principles but will not impose them or injure others in their name. (58)

There is a subtle difference between the authentic impulses rising within us that shape our actions and the conditioned fears that cause us to try to control the actions of other people. Our own convictions energize us and form a stable platform for our decisions. Our attempts to control others, however, exhaust us and cause us to forget our primary identity.

- Notice how your own convictions, positive things themselves, can turn to judgment of others.

I guide my own actions . . . not others.

288

One who follows this path will be honest but never cruel. (58)

Honesty is an often misused and misunderstood quality. We see it used as a weapon in the polite warfare of passive-aggressive sniping and veiled criticism. Seeing and speaking clearly is an art that is carefully cultivated. Kindness must trump honesty if there is a conflict between the two.

- Instead of the word *honesty*, perhaps the phrase "seeing clearly" might be more helpful. How might that change your approach?

I want to see myself and others . . . clearly and with kindness.

289

One who follows this path will be a guide to people but will never overshadow them. (58)

When people turn to us for advice, we face the temptation to place ourselves in a "one up" position. It is a subtle impulse that assumes that we know what is best for them. This skews our relationship and separates us from the power and joy of interdependence and mutual support.

- It's probably best to avoid advice altogether. If advice seems necessary, make sure the relationship is supportive and interdependent.

I have no need . . . to give advice.

290

Moderation is the best way to care for our affairs. It frees us from fixed plans that waste our power. (59)

It seems logical that fixing a plan in our mind and "going after it" would produce results. Many self-help books promote ideas along this line. But keeping our needs moderate helps us see the twists and turns in the path. We can adjust our actions accordingly and arrive safely without exhausting ourselves in futile pressure. We achieve goals without bringing harm to others.

- *Great Expectations* is a good name for a Dickens novel, but not a good strategy for a happy life. What are your great expectations? Can you release them?

I desire . . . a modest and joyful life.

291

We never punish ourselves for things we do or don't do. (59)

When the day unfolds with broken resolutions, wasted time, and doubts that we can ever actually get our lives together, we are face-to-face with the marvelous opportunity that can change everything. If we refuse to entertain any thought of internal criticism, self-punishment, or despair, we will take a giant step into freedom. We will truly feel the Tao within us.

- Those moments are key. When you face them and choose to love yourself, you have won the battle.

I refuse . . . to punish myself.

292

We can respond to the shifting winds of life and use everything for good. (59)

What is happening in life today is a given. How we choose to interpret what is happening is the key to the door of contentment. A painful event can be accepted and used as fuel for courage. A disappointment can be accepted and used to generate deeper insight. A failure can be accepted and used as a signal for a change in direction. An achievement can be celebrated with joy.

- Difficult is difficult, but you can handle difficult. You can handle anything.

I can deal with . . . anything.

293

Deeply rooted in our practice, we never become confused or lose our way. (59)

Of course we sometimes feel lost. Life has turns and twists to which we must adapt, and that will take time and patience. It helps to remember that, underneath the confusion and lost feelings, there is a path on which we walk that will reemerge from the fog soon. Confusion is often just our conditioned mind trying to grasp the ungraspable.

- Confusion is always on the surface. Remember the deeper currents of your life and return to them.

I trust . . . the deep currents of my life.

294

We take care of our most important affairs in the same way we fry a small fish. We don't force the issue. We don't hurry the process. (60)

Conventional wisdom insists that we must be unceasing in our efforts to promote ourselves and our dreams. After all, we are told, no one else will do it for us. In truth, most of the processes of life occur outside of our efforts. We take some action, but only at the proper time and only that which is necessary. Dreams fulfill themselves.

- Let the heat cook your fish. Stop poking it.

I am patient . . . with the process.

295

Our conditioned thoughts of worry and doubt have lost their power. We still notice them arising, but they no longer run our lives. (60)

When our minds fall into the well-worn ruts of fear and worry, our vital energy is wasted. It can't create the life of freedom we seek. It can't guide us with wisdom and clarity. It has too much to do just processing the worries and anticipating fear-filled futures. Worry is not planning. We don't need to follow these thoughts.

- Where are you placing your mental energy today?

What . . . me worry?

296

Because we walk along this path, that which used to make us suffer has been transformed into wisdom. (60)

All the things that make life "difficult" can be turned into spiritual exercises. Patiently working with these things strengthens our confidence and courage. Even when these things seem to overwhelm us, we learn that being overwhelmed is simply one more thing we can handle. We can actually survive being "overwhelmed."

- There is nothing you can't handle. Even death will bring you serenity. What is bringing you wisdom today?

I am capable . . . of all my life.

297

A country settled in this path is like a fertile valley. All the world flows to it and finds a place of rest and welcome. Its stillness and tranquility overcome the restlessness around it and all find lasting peace. (61)

Grabbing and getting are the ways that culture seems to work and our country becomes unwelcoming and hostile. How sad. Shoving and pushing exhaust us. Getting is not the way of the Tao. Receiving is the way of the Tao. If we remain still and cease striving to get ahead, we and all those around us will find what we seek. Our country will be transformed into a thriving place of peace.

- What are you grabbing for? Stop. Open your hands and let it come to you.

I live . . . with open hands.

298

We flourish, not by pretending to be grand but by making a welcoming space for all. (61)

Just because everyone else is rushing and striving doesn't mean we have to join them in the rush. We can choose a slower pace and take the time to watch the clouds drift by. The space we open up will be filled with grateful friends and wonderful experiences. Notice how lovely it is to be in the company of people who are at peace with themselves.

- Grandiosity does not bring us true friends. Spaciousness does.

I have room . . . for true friendship.

299

This path is the source of all that is. It is the refuge of those who follow it. It is the protector of those who ignore it. (62)

The Tao has no "special people." It is neither flattered nor offended by what we and others do. It is available to everyone, always. We love this path because it is that which supports us. But it also supports all those who know nothing about it. That causes us to love it even more because we are free from the need to argue and convince others. We can be who we are. They can be who they are.

- There is never a need to evangelize. Share gently if you wish, but if people ignore you, no problem.

We all . . . belong.

300

We honor those who show no interest in this path with gentle words and loving-kindness. (62)

We prefer to be with people who see the world as we do. That can be a dangerous habit, for we become narrow in our vision and subject to confirmation bias. If we allow in only that which fits our opinions, we miss out on much. Making friends with those who do not share our beliefs will be of great benefit to us and to our new friends. We don't have to pretend to think or believe certain things. We only have to listen and connect at a deeper level than opinion and belief.

- How can you open your circle? You don't have to agree with them. Just treat them with respect.

I learn from . . . those who disagree.

301

Action on this path unfolds without effort.
Work is accomplished without strain.
Life is enjoyed without clinging. (63)

We have been taught that everything in life is "about us." This gives the work we do a stressful edge. We feel that we must achieve this and that to be valued, to be safe. What if our work is not about this thing called "us"? What if it were simply something flowing through us? We do it, but it isn't about us. Consider this.

- Live your life today without it being about you. Enjoy it.

It's not . . . about me.

302

The smallest things are honored and the greatest things are seen as ordinary. (63)

Great things are honored by society. Media craves our attention and attains it by touting great events and people. This subtly keeps us dissatisfied with our own lives. But small things are what bring happiness and contentment. It is the taste of our coffee, the touch of a breeze, and the song of a cardinal in the palo verde tree that we truly want.

- Treat the smallest things today as having the greatest value.

I value most . . . the smallest things.

303

Small steps lead to great accomplishments. Therefore, we pay complete attention to the task in front of us. (63)

What is happening right at this moment? I am sitting at a table writing these words. You are reading these words. I am not writing a book. You are not reading a book. We are simply being with these few words, right here, right now. That is all. Time disappears. Space disappears. We inhabit the eternal present.

- Don't get ahead of yourself. Be here, now!

I am here . . . it is now.

304

Sitting still allows us to notice the subtle stirrings of the mind. Small thoughts that lead to suffering are easily seen and set aside. (64)

Trying to be "good meditators" is a silly waste of time. Meditation is simply being still in any "now" moment when we are seeing, but not believing, any of our thoughts. A certain practice of stillness allows us to become proficient at this process, but it is a process that we can apply at any time.

- Notice what you think. Let it go.

I let my thoughts . . . come and go.

305

This practice seems so passive and still, yet it is the seedling from which the great tree grows. It is the single small step that begins the journey of one thousand miles. (64)

The only step possible is the one that is right in front of us. It is wise to put all our attention on that particular step. If we look ahead we might stumble. A skillful golfer is always, only, playing one shot. A writer is always, only, writing one word. A match is won and a book is finished one small step at a time.

- What are you doing right now? Do only that.

I do . . . only this.

306

We lay down our wanting and pick up our contentment. We lay down our conditioning and pick up our true nature. (64)

We do a great deal of "laying down" on this path. Our culture's economy is predicated on continually wanting something; thus, it is a culture of continual dissatisfaction. We achieve something or get something and immediately want or need something else. We don't need new methods for "getting what we want." We need new techniques for understanding the "wanting" process so we are no longer trapped by it.

- What do you want? Why? Is there a "want" you can let go of?

I want . . . to want less.

307

Great teachers of this path taught with humble simplicity. No cathedrals, no books, no ado at all. Just one person talking to another about ordinary life. (65)

We tend to look for well-known teachers who gather large crowds. We assume they must be saying something important and worthwhile. Hitler drew massive crowds. Politicians of all sorts draw crowds, not by speaking truth but by exciting fears and desires. There are unsung teachers and guides waiting quietly for the student and pilgrim to appear.

- Who are your teachers? Find a teacher who speaks or writes quietly, individually, and without agenda. Listen to them.

I am taught . . . by quiet wisdom.

308

Today the experts babble about everything under the sun, seeking to gather crowds and control circumstances by their clever words. Everyone is cheated. (65)

Zen teacher Shunryu Suzuki said, "In the beginner's mind there are many possibilities. In the expert's mind there are only a few." This path celebrates "beginner's mind." Each moment is new and the possibilities are endless. Expertise is a dangerous thing. It spins an illusion of knowing everything. Experts easily fall into the illusion that they control things because of their knowledge.

- Each moment is new. Forget what you think you know and begin again.

I am . . . a beginner in each moment.

309

All forms and all beings express the power of the Tao by the fullness of their life, and then return to their source. The heart of our teaching is to live in fullness and return in joy. (65)

A full life is a life composed of full moments. A full life is not one of great accomplishments. It is one composed of millions of packed-full moments. Each moment is experienced with complete attention on small, ordinary occurrences. The gradual accumulation of such moments leads unfailingly to joy and to a graceful willingness to return.

- Are you ready to return in joy? If not, begin to fill your moments.

I fill . . . each moment.

310

Streams and rivers carve ravines and canyons because they flow down to the ocean. Their power is in their downward flow. (66)

Life can seem an endless uphill slog. This is an unfortunate image that robs us of our joy. The phrase "It's all downhill from here" is very misleading. It should not be a statement of resignation. It is really an expression of "Whee! Let's ride the toboggan all the way with our arms in the air and the wind in our faces!"

- Stop struggling. How can you enjoy the ride today? It will be over soon.

I love . . . the ride!

311

One who leads us on this path follows along behind. Therefore, our own true nature leads. (66)

Leaders are supposed to be carriers of water to the ones doing the work. It is their job to empower each of us, support us, and get the heck out of our way. They should be unknown. When the job is done, we are able to say, “Look what we were able to do all by ourselves!”

- What kind of leadership do you bring to your job? To your family and friends?

I lead . . . from behind.

312

Our gratitude to the countless beings who have transmitted this path down to the present day is without limit. They taught with gentleness and grace. Few of their names are known. Great is their honor. (66)

It is appropriate that we feel a sense of gratitude to all those throughout history whose quiet, unsung, unnoticed lives have built the foundation on which we rest today. They made mistakes, suffered, learned, and persevered. We are the beneficiaries of a near-infinite cloud of ancestors, literal and spiritual, stretching back to the very beginnings of beginning-less time.

- Take a moment of silence and think of the countless souls whose lives and courage throughout time enabled you to live.

I honor . . . all ancestors.

313

No one sees anything special about this path. No one has been able to market it. No one has trivialized it. (67)

No-thing to buy. No-thing to sell. No-thing to find. No-thing to lose. No-thing to do. No-thing to not do. Notice that there is a difference between "nothing" and "no-thing." No-thing is undifferentiated being, pure awareness, essential consciousness, beyond separate "things." This is us! But in our economy, "things" are paramount because they can be sold. On this path, nothing is bought or sold.

- You are really no-thing. Isn't that wonderful! No need to grasp or cling.

I am . . . no-thing.

314

Wherever there is compassion, fear does not abide. If we try to be fearless but do not have compassion, we become ruthless. (67)

The bold and fearless in our society receive our honor, regardless of the wreckage they leave in their wake. We love our champions and our "number ones" so much that I sometimes wonder if there is any purpose for the rest of us. Politicians bluster and push and shove in order to show their "strength." However, true fearlessness can only exist where compassion lives.

- What are you afraid of? Where is love?

In love . . . fear does not abide.

315

Wherever there is simplicity, generosity abides. If we try to be generous and do not have simplicity, we become controlling. (67)

Philanthropy and charity are honored in our culture, perhaps rightly so. It's better than miserliness, I suppose. But amid the hoopla of ostentatious giving and tax write-offs, we are right to ask not how much is given but *how much is left?*

- You remember the story of the widow's mite? How much do you really need? Why not give the rest?

I live simply . . . so I can be generous.

316

Wherever there is patience, all things are accomplished. If we try to accomplish things but do not have patience, we become failures. (67)

With enough pounding and enough force we can eventually force a square peg into a round opening. So what? We have ruined both the peg and the opening. If we are patient, we may find a peg that fits, or even better, we may realize that this pounding of pegs into holes is a really silly thing to be doing in the first place. How much modern work is exactly this?

- What have you been trying to force? If you are quiet and still, the way ahead will reveal itself.

I sit and wait . . . until the way appears.

317

When someone opposes us, we do not give in to anger. (68)

Anger, in one sense, is a natural emotion, but if it is the energy behind our responses, we will generate an ever-increasing cycle of opposition. Anger will be met with defensiveness and then with more anger, and constructive action will be lost. If we let anger rise and fade, opposition will become constructive, informing and modifying our actions, making them more effective.

- What seems to be opposing you right now? How can it be helpful?

Opposition . . . is just another teacher.

318

We view no one as a competitor because we do not seek our own way. (68)

The need to impose our own ideas on the rest of the world limits life. The continuous game of win or lose implies that only winners matter. "We're number one!" means that healthy diversity must disappear and that different skills and talents become classified as "losers." Spectator sports have a dangerous edge to them when this mindset becomes dominant.

- Do you really have to win? Why? What would happen if you didn't?

My way . . . and your way . . . together.

319

We know our strengths and we know our weaknesses. We use them each for benefit. (68)

We don't have to pretend. Acknowledging and understanding our weaknesses as well as our strengths allows us to structure our activities effectively. We can use our weaknesses to help us connect with others by asking for assistance. Weaknesses foster cooperation if we can honestly and mindfully use them—not putting ourselves down but simply asking for cooperation and assistance.

- Where do you need help? See it as an opportunity.

I know what I can . . . and cannot do.

320

We are not trying to fix ourselves or others, so we move naturally and easily along our path. (68)

Any fixing that is needed will occur naturally as we and others pay attention to the path that unfolds before us. Adjustments can be made without resistance when we stop trying to arrange ourselves and others to fit our ideas of what should be. Improvement can be a good thing, but only when it emerges naturally and not as a result of trying to "fix."

- Are you trying to make adjustments to someone? What if you relaxed and let things unfold?

I don't need to fix . . . anyone.

321

So we move forward without conquering anyone. We gain without anyone losing. (69)

Culture imposes a sense of urgency upon everything we do, so we elbow, push, and trample our way through life. Where are we going that we should be in such haste to get there? What if there is nowhere to get to? What if there is nothing we need to win? What if people are not "in our way" but simply "on the way"?

- Where are you going in such a hurry?

I am in no hurry . . . I don't need to win.

322

We confront obstacles without using weapons. (69)

Do you remember the phrase "mutually assured destruction"—MAD, for short? It refers to the doctrine that atomic war can be deterred because each side would be able to annihilate the other regardless. Truly a MAD doctrine that may indeed destroy us. Weapons destroy. That is their purpose. It seems idealistic, but we know in our hearts that we must find another way. Why not try?

- What do you need to truly protect yourself?

I can protect . . . without destroying.

323

We call no one enemy, for to have an enemy is to lose our inner unity. (69)

Our enemies are truly part of our own existence. They are not separate from us, no matter how distant they seem. We must heal the rift between us as soon as possible and return to unity. It is only the illusion of separateness that allows us to kill them from afar and keeps us huddling in fear.

- Do you have enemies? How can you heal that wound?

An enemy is . . . a part of me.

324

When conflict arises, we refuse to separate ourselves. This is how we remain at peace. (69)

If a person is stronger than we are and is determined to harm us, they will do so, and so bring harm to themselves as well. If we remain at peace, the conflict is far more likely to be resolved without harm to either of us. There is nothing wrong with defending ourselves, but this self-defense is most effective when we are not separate but are essentially "one with" our opponent.

- Who are you in conflict with? Choose to stay connected with them. Don't let the conflict win.

I refuse . . . to be separate.

325

Our conditioned ways of seeing things and doing things make it hard for us to understand, but this path is easy to find and easy to follow. (70)

We've heard this throughout the *Tao Te Ching*: this is not a difficult practice. Our conditioned mind, however, has great difficulty accepting the idea that it is not difficult. Spiritual paths should, it tells us, be followed only with great difficulty and sacrifice. Everything worthwhile, it tells us, is difficult. Although it is true that some things are indeed difficult, walking this path is not one of them.

- When this practice feels difficult to you, stop. See what happens next.

I walk this path . . . without strain.

326

This path arises from the source of all. If we learn to know this source, we learn to know ourselves. (70)

We are not discovering esoteric truths about the structure of the universe. We are finding truths about ourselves in everything we do and in everything that happens. The secrets of the quantum structure of reality are of interest to physicists. The secrets we hide from ourselves are the treasures we seek. Knowing ourselves, we know the Tao. Knowing the Tao, we know ourselves.

- You know yourself better than you'll admit. What are you hiding from yourself?

I want to know . . . my own hidden secrets.

327

Our outer trappings remain simple so we are free to cherish our inner joy. (70)

The idea of simplicity circles around and around in our practice. It has countless facets that reveal themselves over time, such as freedom from meaningless work and freedom from excessive worry over possessions. But the greatest benefit might be the inner happiness and contentment that has always waited within our hearts but been hidden by outer accumulation.

- What are you waiting for? Be happy.

I cherish . . . inner joy.

328

If we pretend to be aware but do not realize our own suffering, we remain ignorant. (71)

Spiritual pretending is a common disease in our culture. Because we've made spirituality one more thing we want to achieve, it is all too easy to check off some boxes and assume the cloak of a spiritual person. Meditation? Check. Devotions? Check. Attend groups? Check. Teach others? Check. Still suffer underneath? There's no reason to pretend. Spirituality is the one place where pretending is not necessary.

- How are you pretending? Don't fool yourself. There's no one watching. Relax.

I see my own suffering . . . I let it go.

329

The fundamental joy of this path is the awareness of the suffering caused by our own mind. Knowing its origin, we know its ending. (71)

We don't have to be afraid of the worries, struggles, and confusions circling around in our minds. It is not necessary to repress them. We don't have to solve them, but we can patiently take the time in quiet stillness to actually see them, understand them, have compassion for them, and then let them fade away. How great is that?

- Don't grasp your mind and try to fix it. Just notice. You'll gradually see how ephemeral your thoughts really are and they will cease lingering.

I understand my thoughts . . . and they fade.

330

If we have no awe of the Mystery, we are easily controlled by fear. (72)

Awe and fear are quite different processes. Their roots are similar, but awe contains the sense of astonishment, amazement, and wonder. Looking at the star-filled sky on a cloudless night is awe-some. We feel small, yet somehow free from the anxiety of our ego games. The universe is too big and too mysterious for that. Awe may have a fearful edge, but not the kind of fear that drives our ego.

- You really are infinitesimally small. Yet you are here, alive, awesome, and in awe. No need to try to control it.

I am small . . . I am free.

331

We constrict ourselves with self-hate and become willing victims of other people. (72)

The constriction of self-hate is one of our conditioned mind's primary strategies for keeping us stuck in mental habits. We forget to value ourselves as part of the Tao and therefore as something truly awesome. We end up listening to anyone who will soothe our fears with subtle words and agendas. We become their unconscious victims because of our need. We forget our intrinsic worth and sovereignty.

- Self-hate is not humility. Just the opposite. Can you sense the difference?

I decide . . . my course in life.

332

We see ourselves clearly but do not become arrogant. We cherish ourselves, but not as separate from all other beings. (72)

When we understand the wondrous blend of our lives as individuals yet also as inseparable from everything else, we can walk that line of clarity without undue pride. Self-love does not become self-obsession or isolation. We can take satisfaction from our accomplishments without separating ourselves from the Whole. We can celebrate ourselves honestly and delight in being a part of all that is.

- Do you see yourself clearly as part of the Whole? Don't be afraid to cherish your life.

I cherish . . . my life.

333

We are only shown the way to walk one step at a time, accepting both harm and benefit as essential parts of life. (73)

One region needs rain and people groan when they see another day of cloudless skies. Another region is flooded and people groan when another day is filled with rain. Since we can't possibly know what is truly beneficial and what is harmful, we may as well accept what is happening now and take the steps that seem best in the moment.

- Don't think about "good" and "bad." Concentrate on seeing clearly what the next step might be.

What is . . . the next step?

334

We are shown how to remain quiet, yet respond to every situation. (73)

Active and receptive are the two poles of walking the Taoist path. Receptivity, cultivated in the quiet stillness of nature walks or simple restful inactivity, is the necessary complement to helpful and effective action. True helpful action grows from within the situation itself, seen only when our mind is quiet enough to perceive. These poles must balance, which in our culture means more quiet, less action.

- If you are facing a situation that requires action, first be quiet. Then, stay quiet. Only then think about acting.

I act . . . from quiet.

335

We are shown how to be patient, yet accomplish everything. (73)

Patience is everything. Urgency permeates the very air we breathe, fueled by our fears, which in turn are stoked by our media. We feel compelled to act, yet have no idea how to take any action that would help. We hurry through every moment of life. Being quiet is essential, but we can't be quiet unless we cultivate patience. We can patiently wait even when the inner voices shout, "Hurry!"

- Be patient. Let the mud settle. See clearly. Then act.

There is . . . no hurry.

336

The mysteries and unknowns along this path are many, yet on it we will never lose our way. (73)

We will never understand enough to settle all our fears and questions. We will never control things well enough to feel completely safe. It is all right to be curious and to explore these mysteries, but we don't really need to know anything but the power of the present moment. Whatever the Mystery might be, we are part of it. Wherever our origin might be, we are returning to it.

- You'll know one day. In the meantime, keep paying attention.

I am not lost . . . I am on the way.

337

Our true nature does not fear death. Our conditioned mind creates this fear in a futile attempt to control events and keep people in line. (74)

There is no way we can convince our conditioned mind that death is acceptable. That mind is anchored in the world of survival instincts. It must try to control the externals of health and safety at all costs. It is willing to kill in order to keep living. Our true nature seeks a balance of survival needs with a deeper sense of unity and oneness.

- Is there a place in your mind where death is accepted?

I accept . . . that death will come.

338

Death is a natural part of this life. An unnatural fear of death leads only to killing. (74)

The centered mind accepts death and uses it to keep attention focused on the precious moments that constantly unfold in mysterious wonder. As it is said, there is nothing like a terminal diagnosis to focus one's attention. If fear takes over, we react like a cornered animal, ready to kill anything perceived as a threat. So many millions of senseless killings are manifestations of this unnatural fear.

- Don't let your fear blind you. Don't let it become hate.

I am . . . not afraid.

339

If we try to use the intricate tools of a master craftsperson, we will cut ourselves. (74)

The Tao is the intelligence that permeates the cosmos. It is manifesting the dance of life and death in each moment. It is both the music and the dance, and its purposes are beyond our comprehension. In working out our own purposes and plans, we must recognize that we are subject to the flow of the Tao and not try to bend it to our will. When we interfere, we always cause harm.

- Are you content with the limitations of a life that is subject to something greater than itself?

I work . . . within the Tao.

340

Why do the poor lack what they need? Because the rich consume too much. (75)

Despite the convoluted concepts of modern economics, the idea that enough is enough remains the basic assumption in following the flow of Tao. Generating a massive amount of wealth is not necessarily contrary to the Tao. However, keeping any of that wealth for ourselves beyond the basic needs for a simple, joyful life is certainly contrary to the Tao.

- How much do you need, really? How much do you keep for yourself?

Wealth . . . is not mine alone.

341

Why do people become restless and discontent? Because those in power try to control every aspect of their lives. (75)

The political system in our culture is based on control. "They" want to impose their views on "us" and will pass horrible laws and do terrible things if they get in power. "We" want to impose our views on "them" and will . . . ? It is the same process. We fail to notice that whoever "they" or "we" are, the fear of being controlled fuels the divisions. Do we really think that controlling others will bring us to peace?

- How do you try to control others—their views and actions? Sure you do. We all do.

I release . . . my control of you.

342

Everyone is so concerned with getting and keeping that no one learns to really live before they die. (75)

We can strive each moment for more security. We can gather distractions by the boatload. We can collect a houseful of toys. Where, in the midst of all this work, do we learn how to really live? Who will tell us when to stop and breathe? What is it really all about?

- When it is your time to die, will you have truly lived?

I want . . . to fully live.

343

To follow this path, we must abandon overconsumption and embrace true simplicity. (75)

Simplicity is the surest security we can build. A life that does no harm to the earth, to others, or to oneself is the most secure of all lives. Even our underlying fear of death is lessened by our ability to live naturally in relationship with the seasons and gifts of the earth. When we feel a part of this marvelous ecosystem, death loses much of its power. The more secure we feel, the less we need to consume.

- This theme repeats often. Are you living naturally and simply with your gifts and resources?

My security lies . . . in my simplicity.

344

Before we are conditioned by all the "dos and don'ts" of life, we are naturally tender and gentle. As we grow old, we constrict around these conditions and end up dying stiff and rigid. (76)

As the rules, opinions, fears, desires, and possessions pile up, our lives become more and more constrained. Everywhere we turn we run into a wall of conditioned thought. Unless we take care to keep our thoughts and our muscles flexible, we will become stiff and brittle of both body and mind. "Abs of steel" may sell gym memberships, but a graceful, supple body will bring life.

- Keep your mind and body supple. Read, do yoga or taiji. Dance. Swim. Live.

My mind is open . . . my body is supple.

345

Indeed, all living things begin soft and supple and end brittle and dry. So we see that hardness and inflexibility are signs of death and that tenderness and gentleness are signs of life. (76)

The athlete whose body is flexible and able to respond quickly to changing situations is the one who is truly alive. Mental muscle obeys the same rules. Hard, rigid minds may give the impression of strength, but they are already dying from lack of movement, suppleness, and flexibility.

- Are you building the kind of strength that lasts? How can you make your thinking more flexible?

My mind and body . . . respond smoothly.

346

It is the ability of an army to change its plans that keeps it from defeat. It is the ability of a tree to bend in the wind that keeps it from toppling. (76)

Our culture calls flexibility being "wishy-washy." It sees a willingness to change course as "unfocused meandering." It calls pausing to rethink our actions "giving up." It requires a courageous willingness to pay close attention to counteract these cultural messages. We have to remember the power of a supple mind.

- Are you supple? Are you overly rigid? How and why?

I can change . . . my course.

347

Our natural tenderness is our true strength. (76)

Tenderness is not a sentimental, mushy quality. It is a powerful energy that can only emerge from a life that is centered and whole. The absence of tenderness in a person is not a sign of strength. False strength can only imitate tenderness in a cloying, artificial way. When our true nature guides us, our strength emerges and tenderness comes with it.

- Are you frightened of tenderness? Does it seem weak to you? Why?

I am strong enough . . . to be tender.

348

Following this path is like stringing a bow and creating a dynamic balance. It encourages a dynamic balance between excess and deficiency. When we see an excess, we decrease it. (77)

We live in a culture that seeks to constantly increase excess through a process of endless growth. Look where that idea has gotten us. Even the idea of "sustainable growth" is contrary to the Tao. Growth must always, in some fashion, give way to decrease. When growth produces excess, decrease is the way of the Tao. Yin replaces yang until balance is restored. A dynamic steady state of production and consumption is the ideal and leads to maximum happiness.

- Watch how this balancing process seeks to work. Can you cooperate with it?

Increase . . . decrease . . . balance . . . happiness.

349

When we see a deficiency, we give to it. (77)

It is all too easy to turn a blind eye to the deficiencies all around us. Millions have no homes, no food, no medical care, and no hope. We cannot, of course, solve the economic and political problems of the world by ourselves. The Tao simply asks that we notice—that we pay attention. This enables us to see where someone lacks something that might correspond to an excess we have. This is our opportunity to move toward balance.

- Don't feel obligated or guilty. Simply see, then do what seems natural.

I see lack . . . I give.

350

To keep balance, we must keep to this path and trust our true nature. This allows us to give without worry and receive without attachment. (77)

When balance is our goal, we are able to give more freely of our excess, not thinking of ourselves as "generous" but as simply enjoying a life in balance. We are also able to receive from others more readily, not feeling "needy" but appreciating the balancing effect of human nature when it operates naturally. No one is either "one up" or "one down" in this process.

- How easily can you give? Perhaps more important, how easy is it for you to receive?

I give . . . I receive.

351

Like water, this path is soft and yielding, yet there is no better way to overcome the stiffness and rigidity that causes so much suffering. (78)

Water's yielding nature allows it to support the entire circle of life. Oceans remain the habitat of millions of species and their waters are the origin of all life on earth. The ocean nurtures every living being. The ocean's waters, through all their wanderings in sky and earth, never fail to return to it. Our bodies are mostly water. Where does the rigidity come from? From our minds.

- You are mostly water. Live that truth in each moment.

I am . . . water.

352

By accepting all that seems humble and plain, we become masters of every situation. (78)

Humility allows us to move within any situation with effectiveness. Blustering displays of muscle and brandishing of armed forces only create enemies and foster constant opposition, in individuals and in nations. The master of a situation sees reality without bombast and bravado, goes unnoticed and therefore penetrates to the heart of things.

- Flexing your muscles, figuratively or literally, only creates opposition. Do you want to look powerful or actually be powerful?

My power comes . . . from humility.

353

Resentment always leads to more resentment. Only contentment leads to contentment. (79)

We cannot resent our way to happiness. We cannot hate our way to joy. The conditioned mind tends to hang on to resentments and other negative thought patterns because they are familiar and easy to reinforce. We believe this will keep us safe. Contentment, though, is a choice, as are all positive patterns. When we choose it, we become open to the thought processes that reinforce it. We begin to see contentment everywhere we turn.

- Which thought patterns will you reinforce?

I choose . . . to see the joy.

354

Our contentment is independent of the actions of others. (79)

Freedom from the opinions and actions of others is freedom indeed. Of course, another person might intrude into our lives in a manner that requires us to take action to protect our personal boundaries. But our boundaries are primarily maintained by our own patterns of thinking, choosing what will and will not be part of the energy system of our brain by carefully curating the input and influence of others to deal with what might be called "energy vampires."

- What people and systems "vampire" your energy? How do you protect yourself?

I decide . . . the content of my mind.

355

Seeking a special position is not the way of life. There are no "special favorites" along this path. It unfolds itself before whoever walks along it. (79)

Most religious traditions, for all their beauty, consider that their particular tradition is somehow composed of "God's favored people." Walking a Taoist path, we are free to believe or disbelieve the tenets of any tradition. We can call ourselves Christians, Muslims, or atheists and still be offered this unfolding path to support us as we explore our lives. We are free from the burden of being "special." And it is a burden.

- No special favorites here. Is that okay?

I walk a path . . . of universal welcome.

356

The present moment is all we have; therefore, we are not constantly seeking a faster way to do things or a better place to be. (80)

If we could manage to calculate the hours we spend trying to earn money to buy things that we think will give us more time for enjoying our life, we might find a surprising conclusion. We work harder than ever in our attempt to make life easier. We go faster than ever in our attempt to get someplace we can enjoy. Say that again? We must have missed something.

- Buy only that which actually delivers on the promise. Do only that which does the same.

I am . . . in no hurry.

357

Our vehicles sit idle except when truly needed and our weapons remain locked away. (80)

In an automobile-obsessed culture, the idea of vehicles sitting idle sounds insane. There are those, however, whose lives do not center around their car(s) or their weapons. They choose to live within walking or biking distance of what they need. They choose public transportation (in those countries that value such transportation). They do not own cars, nor do they depend on weapons. They are willing to give up so-called convenience and independence for a greater good and a more satisfying life.

- What is your relationship with automobiles? Does it need shifting?

I walk . . . I bike . . . I share the road.

358

Our attention is always on the experience of the moment, so we enjoy our food, our clothing, our homes, and every aspect of a simple way of living. (80)

Good food is gobbled in front of screens. Good drink is guzzled while watching football. Comfortable homes and warm clothing are taken for granted while our attention wanders to and fro. So many do not have the basic human pleasures of food, shelter, and clothing while many of us don't notice that we have it all.

- Don't feel guilty. Pay attention to the food, drink, and comfort! If you understand how blessed you are, it will increase the likelihood of generosity.

I savor the joys . . . of my life.

359

Though the world is filled with sights we haven't seen, we die content because we have truly lived. (80)

Bucket lists have a romantic sound, but they seem to indicate a tendency to postpone living. Living is what is happening while we're thinking about something else. Living is not the extraordinary moments. Living is the millions of ordinary sights, sounds, touches, tastes, and aromas that drift past our attention unnoticed. If the ordinary is attended to, the extraordinary will take care of itself.

- Enjoy the moments. They pass in a blink. They are never ordinary.

I attend . . . each moment.

360

The most helpful words do not please our conditioning. Words that please our conditioning are not helpful. (81)

Our conditioning selects only familiar words and images. It avoids new information, new ways of doing things, and new ideas. The familiar is seen as safe. However, each day the breezes on this path reveal something new and fresh. To allow this fresh air to blow through our lives, we must not let our conditioned mind shut the doors and windows.

- Are you surfing the same old ideas? Reading the same old stuff? Comfortable, yes. But stale.

I open my life . . . to fresh breezes.

361

This path is not taught by argument. Those who argue are not teaching this path. (81)

Argument is somewhat different from discussion, though we frequently imply the same thing with either word. “Let me show you how wrong you are and how right I am” tends to be the goal of argument or discussion. But if we are, indeed, so right, what need is there to show someone? We can speak of what we see, but we can’t make someone else see what we see. They will see their own way ahead.

- Never argue a spiritual path. You will distort the path itself.

I see . . . but never argue.

362

Books cannot teach this path. If we rely on books, we will not find this path. (81)

We read the *Tao Te Ching* and find occasional encouragement, occasional discouragement, and frequent puzzlement. The book is not the Tao. Books, for all their benefit, can't help but attempt to contain, explain, and control concepts—a futile task. We can have pity for poor writers who try to write the Tao. It can't be done. Treat them gently, they do their best.

- At best a book is a finger pointing at the moon. Forget the finger. See the moon.

I see . . . the moon.

363

Simplicity is our joyous and practical guide. Therefore, we always have enough to live with generosity. (81)

A person has two dollars left in their pocket from their entertainment budget. They are heading to a coffee shop where they will spend it on a luscious cookie. They pass a homeless woman huddled on the curb. They are tired of the homeless cluttering up downtown. They ignore her and pass by. Then . . . they turn around, walk back, and give her the two dollars. Their generosity surpasses that of Bill and Melinda Gates.

- No one cares how much you give. The question once again is, how much do you keep?

I have enough . . . to share.

364

This path brings great gain, yet does not harm. (81)

So much of what our culture has "gained" over the millennia has caused harm in so many ways. We gained a land by harming and dispossessing native inhabitants. We have gained convenience by harming the ecosystem, possibly beyond repair. The Taoist ideal is to balance any gain we might achieve against any possible harm we might do. How might this ideal change our economic life? Can we learn to gain without harming?

- What have you gained in your life? Has it caused unintentional harm?

I gain . . . without doing harm.

365

No longer striving for control, we find life to be an ever-flowing river. (81)

Water is the ultimate description of the Tao. As Alan Watts said, the Tao is "The Watercourse Way." It is not a spiritual ascent up steep mountain paths, nor is it an austere survival trek through arid deserts. Its course may take us through all sorts of terrain, but it is first and foremost a river flowing unfailingly to its home. We are that river. We will reach home.

- Let go. Let it flow. Use your paddle to guide your boat, not to row upstream. Life is a dream. (Listen to a recording of Pete Seeger singing "River of My People.")

I am the river . . . flowing home.

Conclusion

Keep going. Start again at the beginning. The *Tao Te Ching* is not a holy book of rock-carved rules. It changes every time you read it because it always speaks to your present moment. You cannot exhaust it. It will be your lifelong companion and champion. I wish you a continued wonderful journey and perhaps I'll see you down the road.

Blessings,
William Martin
Somewhere in the southern Arizona desert, July 2023
www.williammartin.org

Appendix

The Complete *Tao Te Ching*

1. Direct Experience
Talking about a path
is not walking that path.
Thinking about life
is not living.

Directly experiencing life
brings unconditional appreciation
and unity.
Thinking about life
brings conditional judgments
and separation.

Free of conditioned thinking,
we experience our true nature.
Caught in conditioned thinking,
we experience only who we think
we are.

Yet both our conditioned nature
and our true nature
are part of life itself.
Our conditioned experience of
living
is a gateway to unconditional life.

---

2. Opposites
Beauty cannot exist
without ugliness.
Virtue cannot exist
without vice.
Living, we know death.
Struggling, we know ease.
Rising high, we know the depths.
Being quiet, we understand noise.

Everything gives rise to its
opposite,
therefore we work without
conscious effort,
and teach without agenda.
We enjoy everything

and possess nothing.
Our accomplishments
do not emerge from our ego,
so we do not cling to them.
Thus they benefit all beings.

---

3. Return to Passion

If achievement is valued,
jealousy will result.
If possessions are valued,
hoarding and stealing will result.

Therefore this path is one
of contentment and simplicity.
It empties the mind of its
chattering,
and fills the soul with truth.
It frees us from our wanting
and returns us to our passion.

No longer needing to have our
own way,
we are not fooled by clever plots
and plans.
Our actions become focused, pure,
and effortless.

---

4. The Bounty of Life

Walking this path,
we experience inexhaustible energy.
From what appears an empty void,
we find the bounty of life.

Our edginess, tension,
anger, and turmoil
begin to settle down.
In their place we find
a deep tranquility
that has been here waiting
since before the beginning
of beginning-less time.

---

5. No Preferences

Life has no preferences.
Every manifestation has its place
and lives its life under the sun.
Therefore we welcome
everything and everyone
without distinction.

Life continuously breathes
its forms into existence,
never depleting itself,
always replenishing itself.

Clinging to our preferences,
we separate ourselves from life
and suffer exhaustion.
Sitting still and following our
breath, we find renewal.

---

6. The Mother of All

Everything that exists was born
of the feminine principle within
the Tao.
This mysterious principle can be
called
"the mother of all."

There is no need

to weary ourselves in an effort to find her.
She is ever with us
because she is us.

---

7. The Watcher

How can we find the eternal,
the lasting nature of the Tao,
that seems so elusive amid the changes of life?

The Tao does not come and go
as do all formations.
It is the watcher of the comings
and the goings.

In our practice we find
that we are the watcher as well.
We watch our opinions and ideas,
our likes and dislikes,
our desires and our fears,
our bodies and our minds,
but we do not identify with them.
Therefore, when they arise,
we watch.
When they pass away,
we remain.

---

8. Our Life Flows Like Water

Our true nature is like water.
It doesn't decide whom to nurture
and whom to avoid.
It doesn't decide that some tasks
are too distasteful.
It just flows like a river to the ocean,
nurturing everything in its path.
This is the nature of the Tao within all people.

Living by this principle,
we choose dwellings that are simple and humble.
We meditate to cultivate quiet
and serene thoughts.
We treat all beings with loving-kindness.
We speak with compassion and clarity.
We manage our lives for the benefit of all beings.
We live in awareness of the present moment
and take action only when the time is right.

In this manner, our life flows like water
and fulfills itself naturally.

---

9. A Path of Letting Go

This is a path of letting go
so there will be room to live.

If we hold on to opinions,
our minds will become dull and useless.
Let go of opinions.

If we hold on to possessions,
we will always be at risk.
Let go of possessions.

If we hold on to ego,
we will continue to suffer.
Let go of ego.

Working without thought of praise or blame
is the way of true contentment.

---

10. According to Our Natural Virtue

Can we embrace both the acceptable
and unacceptable parts of ourselves?
Can we breathe as easily as innocent babies?
Can we see the world clearly
and without judgment?
Can we act with loving-kindness
yet remain unknown and unsung?
Can we watch all things come and go,
yet remain undisturbed?
Can we accept our countless thoughts and opinions,
yet not take them seriously?

If we can do this we are acting
according to the virtue that is naturally ours;
nourishing all things, but possessing nothing;
enjoying all things, but clinging to nothing;
working diligently,
but claiming credit for nothing;
growing in wisdom, but controlling nothing.

---

11. Intangible and Invisible Within Us

The spokes and the hub
are the visible parts of a wheel.
The wheel is useful because it spins about
the invisible point at its center.

Clay is the material from which a pot is made.
The pot is useful because of the empty space inside the form.

A house is made with walls, doors, and windows.
The house becomes a home for people
through the quality of life lived within.

We practice with the visible and tangible,
but it is the invisible and intangible within us
that bring us life.

---

12. Mysterious and Internal

Trying to see everything,
we become blind.
Listening to every voice,
we become confused.
Attempting to satisfy all our appetites
we become weary.
Being driven this way and that
by our conditioning
makes us crazy.
Buying more things
only wastes our energy.

Outer things exist,
but do not define us.
We are mysterious and internal
not obvious and external.

13. All Things as Ourselves

Expecting either praise or blame
makes us anxious.
Seeing ourselves as separate and isolated
makes us suffer.

What are the implications of
"expecting either praise or blame
makes us anxious"?
To desire praise is to fear blame.
To fear blame is to desire praise.
Both are rooted in fear
and bound up in desire.
That is why on this path
there is neither praise nor blame.

What are the implications of
"seeing ourselves as separate and isolated
makes us suffer"?
We are all expressions of the one life
of the Tao.
Seeing ourselves as separate is a mistake
that leaves us feeling vulnerable.
We use countless strategies
to protect ourselves from this vulnerable feeling.
This is the root of our suffering.

Knowing that we are part of everything that is,
we care for and nurture all things as ourselves.

14. Return to Our Breath

What we are seeking
can't be seen, heard, or touched.
It is our essential unity
beyond the divisions of our senses.

It is not obvious to the mind,
but neither is it hidden from the heart.

Looking at nothing,
all of a sudden there it is!
But the moment we see it, it disappears,

leaving only a vague memory.

Chasing after it is useless
because it didn't begin anytime
and isn't going anywhere.
To realize our true nature,
we need only return to our breath,
here and now.

15. The Freedom of Enlightenment

The freedom of enlightenment
is impossible to describe.
We can only notice how it appears in action.

We pay complete attention
to whatever we are doing,
as if we were crossing a river
on ice-covered stones.
We are alert to everything that happens,
like a bird watching in all directions.
We have a quiet dignity and reserve,
like a guest who does not seek attention.
Our judgments and opinions have melted away,
like ice in the summer heat.
There is a beautiful simplicity about us,
like a gem before it is shaped and polished.
We welcome whatever comes,
as a valley welcomes the river.

To notice this enlightenment,
we sit patiently and wait
for muddy thoughts to settle
and our mind to become clear.
Life then lives itself in us.

Practicing this path, we no longer worry
about what we have or don't have
because we have everything!

16. The Still Point

When the chatter of our mind quiets down,
we find the still point
around which all of life revolves.
From this still point we watch everything
come and go in perfect peace.

Everything that is, was, or ever will be
has a common source from which it comes,
in which it lives,
and to which it returns.

Understanding this coming and going,
we return to our source and our confusion ends.

Not understanding this, we remain
confused
and bring about great suffering.

Living at the still point, we are
open to all of life.
Open to all of life, we don't judge
anything.
Not judging, we see with
compassion.
Seeing with compassion,
we discover our true nature.
Discovering our true nature,
we are at home
and nothing in life disturbs us.

17. It Happened Naturally

The deepest virtue is to be unaware
of a separate self at all.
Being aware of a separate self,
it is good to have compassion for
that self.
Not having compassion for our
self,
we become afraid of our own
nature.
Being afraid of our own nature,
we come to actually hate our self.
Hating our self,
how can we value anyone else?

Free from self-hate,
our actions are not burdened
by our need for attention.
Therefore people say,
"It happened naturally."

18. A Pretense of Life

When we forget who we truly are,
we turn to external rules
to define goodness and morality.
When we no longer live from our
heart,
we search for clever strategies
to guide our actions.
This is only a pretense of life.

Duty and loyalty become
substitutes
for our inability to love ourselves
and others.
Then we insist our leaders heal the
suffering
created by our own divided minds.

19. Our True Nature Waiting

If we give up our attempts to
be holy and wise, everyone,
including ourselves,
will greatly benefit.
If we give up our rules for goodness
and justice,
all beings will naturally be treated
with loving-kindness.
If we give up striving to
accumulate by clever means,
theft will disappear.

But these lessons are mere outward
forms.

The core of our path is this:
we see through our
conditioned mind
and find our true nature waiting.

---

20. Whatever Comes Your Way

We always strive to make the right choice,
and always fear the wrong choice.
We pursue what others say is good,
and avoid what others say is bad.
How sad this is for us!
People are constantly stirred up
like children at a circus—
always looking for the next act to entertain them.
But this practice asks us to remain undisturbed,
and watch all things
with the detached interest of a newborn.

In a culture where excess accumulation is the norm,
this path seems idiotic.
Fearful voices in our mind warn us
that we will end up wandering the street,
homeless and alone.
We are urged to be clever and successful
and always in control.
But this practice asks us to relinquish the illusion of control
and to be content with whatever comes our way.

This seems so strange
and different from the usual way.
But it is the way of life itself.

---

21. By Being It

This path brings us to our true nature.

Though this way seems elusive
and avoids our words and concepts,
it is the source of everything
seen and unseen.

Though walking this path
seems to take us into deep
and hidden shadows,
it leads us into the very
life force of all things.
Since before the beginning
of beginning-less time,
it has been both creator of,
and witness to, all existence.

We know the truth of this way,
not by believing it,
but by being it.

---

22. The Only Path to Wholeness

Accepting what is, we find it to be perfect.
What seemed distorted is seen as true.

What seemed lacking is seen as abundant.
What seemed worn out is seen as fresh and new.

Possessing little, we are content.
Too much stuff and we lose our way.

When we reside at the center,
our actions nurture all things.
We don't act out of ego needs,
so our actions are enlightened.
We don't claim to be perfect,
so our ideas are welcomed.
We aren't looking for reward,
so our teaching is enduring
and accessible to all.
We don't try to control or convince anyone,
so opposition is not an issue.

"Accept what is,
and find it to be perfect"
is not an idle phrase.
Acceptance of life
is the only path to wholeness.

---

23. A Seamless Joyful Whole

This is a path of few words.
Silence is the natural way of life.
Strong winds arise,
and pass away.
Torrential rains arise,
and pass away.
Even the cosmos,
which produces the wind and rain,
passes away.
Why then so much concern
over what to do
and what to say?

Our life is an expression of life itself.
Our true nature expresses itself
in everything we do.
Success and failure are seen
as part of a seamless joyful whole.
Each is accepted
and fully lived.

---

24. Until We Lay It Down

Stretching to reach it,
we fall.
Running to catch it,
we get lost.
Pretending to be enlightened,
we become dim and foolish.
Trying to "do it right,"
we fail.
Looking for praise,
we receive nothing.
Grabbing hold of it,
we lose it.

All of this strutting, striving,
straining, and grasping
is excess baggage.

The very freedom it promises does
not appear
until we lay it down.

---

25. Our True Home
This path we follow existed
before the universe was born.

It contains within itself
unchanging tranquility and
solitude.
It is present wherever we turn
and provides inexhaustible
compassion
to all beings.
Thus it may be considered
the mother of the universe.
It has no name, but if we have to
refer to it we call it Tao.

It can also be called the great
mystery
from which we come, in which
we live,
and to which we return.

It is a path filled with the
grandeur
of the cosmos, the earth,
and the human heart.

This path is our true home
because it is home to all things
in heaven and on earth.

---

26. Why Scurry About?
Because this path is deeply rooted,
it allows us to be lighthearted
and not take ourselves too
seriously.
Because this path is stable,
it allows us to act without rashness.

So, whatever we do,
we do not abandon ourselves.
Even though the world provides
endless worries and distractions,
we remain unconcerned and
content.

We have everything we could
want.
Why would we scurry about
looking for something else?
Only if we lose touch with our true
nature
are we trapped in agitation and
hurry.

---

27. The Great Secret
This path has no rules, no rituals,
and no preconceived notions.
Traveling it we seek neither praise
nor blame,
yet our actions become impeccable
and blameless.

Our life is illumined by the light.
Everything that happens
is for our benefit.

Everything in our experience
instructs us in the way.
Everyone we meet becomes our teacher,
good and bad alike.
Everyone we meet becomes our student,
bright and dull alike.
If we try to pick and choose,
we will never learn.

Ceasing to pick and choose:
this is the great secret of life.

28. For the Benefit of All

Striving to make our way in the world
seems prudent.
But if we trust our heart
we may find the way opening
with the effortless ease
of a budding flower.

Striving to live a life of virtue
is approved of by all.
But if we trust our heart
we may find the power of our true nature
everywhere we turn,
in everyone we meet.

Charismatic personalities
capture our attention.
But it is our true nature,
existing beneath our personality,
that brings power and purpose to our life.

Separate from our true nature,
we create forms and functions
and struggle to make them work.
Returning to our original nature,
we use the forms and functions
for the benefit of all.

29. Control Is an Illusion

Attempting to control external events
will never keep us safe.
Control is an illusion.

Whatever we try to control,
we separate from ourselves.
Whatever we try to fix,
we ruin.
Life is sacred,
and flows exactly as it should.

We return to our breathing.
It knows exactly what to do,
rising and falling without conscious control.
In the same way
we sometimes have an excess
and sometimes have a lack.
We sometimes assert ourselves,
and sometimes hold back.
We sometimes succeed,
and sometimes fail completely.

Our practice is to see all this
without taking it seriously.

That way we do not abandon
ourselves.
We remain at peace.

30. Focused and Effective

Practicing this path,
we do not struggle.
To struggle is to invite resistance.
To invite resistance is to create
suffering in our life,
and in the world.

Paying attention to the present
moment,
we see the things that we must do.
We do them without complaint,
resistance,
or second-guessing,
then we stop.
We don't complicate our actions
by seeking control or recognition.

Correct action, however difficult,
is naturally focused and effective.
Adding struggle complicates
and does not lead to lasting good.

31. Weep That This Has Happened

Weapons of violence
are contrary to the common good,
no matter how skillfully used.
So we vow to do no harm.

Faced with unavoidable violence
we remember this vow,
act quickly,
and return immediately to peace.

Battles are not with "enemies"
but with beings like ourselves.
Knowing this, we do not rejoice in
victory
nor take delight in the downfall of
others.
Victory is an illusion and gains us
nothing.

Once a battle is over we lay our
weapons down
and weep that this has happened.

32. We Return to Peace

What we call the Tao
really has no name.
Naming something, we think we
understand it.
What we call the Tao is far too
subtle for that.
We experience it in our own true
nature.
If we hold on to our own true
nature,
all external and internal strife falls
away.
Peace descends on our lives
like a gentle rain from heaven.

Joy flows from the earth
like a mighty river.
There is no need to urge ourselves
to do good.
Goodness is our heart's true
nature.

The more we use words,
the more distinctions we make.
The more distinctions we make,
the more we suffer.
When we stop taking distinctions
seriously,
we cease to suffer.
We return to peace
just as streams and rivers
return to the ocean.

---

33. Adequate for Our Life

Studying other people
brings us knowledge.
Studying our own mind
brings us freedom.
Overcoming other people
requires force.
Overcoming our conditioning
requires true power.
Once we realize that we
always have
everything we need,
we understand that we are truly
adequate for our life.

Identifying with our true
nature,
we also discover that we are
adequate
for our death as well.

---

34. The Greatness That We Are

The great Tao is like an ocean.
It fills the universe
and all things rely upon it.
It gives us birth
and never abandons us.

It does all this marvelous work
and needs no recognition.
It nourishes and sustains us
yet does not claim to own us.
It has no need for glory
so it blends into the background
and is hardly ever noticed.
It is the true home to which we
return,
yet it wants no worship.
No wonder we consider it great.

Our own greatness doesn't come
from power or control.
We just live our lives each moment
as the greatness that we are.

---

35. We Turn to This Path

Our practice looks beneath
the passing thoughts that seem so
real.
Clinging to them brings pain.
Letting them come and go
brings peace.

Lively music and good food
may capture our attention,
but speaking of this path
is not exciting.
People would rather try to make
things work,
look for distractions,
and listen to empty promises.

We turn to this path
only when we have exhausted
all other paths.

36. This Is the Secret of Our Path

If we try to get rid of something,
it will naturally remain.
If we try to weaken a habit,
it will naturally remain strong.
If we try to push away our
thoughts,
they will naturally return.
If we try to get rid of our pain,
we will suffer all the more.

This is the secret of our path:
gentleness and flexibility
bring the results
that force and rigidity
fail to achieve.

Our true benefit lies
not in our words or arguments,
but in the depth of our practice.

37. As If We Do Nothing

Our practice is one of
effortless effort.
It seems as if we do nothing,
yet everything is done.

If we stay on this path
and resist the temptation to
control,
each thing will naturally evolve
according to its individual nature.

When our conditioning arises
and attempts to stir us up,
we return to the simple stillness
of our natural state.
When we abide at this still point
our conditioned habits naturally
fall away,
leaving only peace.

38. Natural Goodness

Not trying to be good,
we experience natural goodness.
Being good, while hoping for
reward,
has nothing to do with natural
goodness.
Natural goodness works effortlessly
and benefits all.
Contrived goodness requires great
effort
and accomplishes very little.
Compassion acts and seeks
nothing.

Justice acts and seeks specific
results.
Morality acts, then demands,
and then forces correct behavior.
When we are separated from our
true nature,
we turn to rules of goodness.
When we fail at being good,
we make more detailed rules
to govern our relationships.
When our relationships suffer,
we insist on justice and fairness.
Not finding justice or fairness,
we all agree to pretend
that empty rituals will suffice.

Our practice is to see through
this artificial effort
and choose to trust in our true
nature.
With that choice, our suffering
ends.

---

39. Dependent on the Tao

With this practice we find
clarity.
Our horizons become expansive.
Our daily life becomes tranquil.
Our souls become inspired.
Our relationships become filled
with trust and honesty.
Our society flourishes.
Everything around us becomes
filled with creative life.

Without this practice we continue
to suffer.
Our horizons contract.
Our daily life fills with anxiety.
Our souls wither.
Our relationships crumble.
Our society flounders.
Everything around us seems
exhausted.

Despite our seeming prestige and
power,
we know that we are really little
children,
dependent on the Tao and helpless
without it.

A wagon rolls along and does
its job
with no fanfare at all.

Rather than clattering about
trying to be noticed,
we just roll along
like common stones in the river.

---

40. A Tender and Gentle Path

Following this path
returns us to our root.
It is a tender and gentle path.

Everything in the cosmos
depends on everything else.
Even our experience of life
depends upon our death.

---

41. Hidden in Silence

The most helpful response to this path
is to devote ourselves to it
and practice it diligently.
But most people practice it only half-heartedly,
and some people disregard it entirely,
seeing it as absurd.
The Tao reflects to us our own inner attitudes.
This is its greatness.

So we can establish a set of helpful maxims:
The way to clarity will seem confusing.
The way to progress
will seem like going backward.
The smoothest way will seem filled with obstacles.
The greatest power will lie in receptivity.
True innocence will appear shameful.
The greatest resources will appear inadequate.
Genuine goodness will appear suspect.
The truly solid and dependable
will seem uncertain.
Effective boundaries will be limitless.
The wisest person will always be learning.

The most pleasing music is hidden in silence.
The most beautiful art begins without form.
And so this path itself, silent and without form,
is the way to all beauty and joy.

---

42. Yin and Yang

Hidden in the mystery of the Tao
lies the original unity.
This unity contains the duality
of yin and yang.
Yin and yang together
produce the energy of creation
and give rise to all things.

Every atom of the cosmos
contains the yin and the yang together.
We feel this harmonious process
in the rising and falling
of our breath.

It seems natural to avoid loss and seek gain,
but on this path such distinctions are not helpful.
There is no gain without loss.
There is no fullness without deprivation.
Who knows how or when

one gives way to the other.
So we remain at the center
and trust events instead of forcing
them.
This is the heart of all spiritual
paths.

---

43. Act Without Ado

The most fluid and yielding
substance
will flow past the most rigid
with the speed of a racehorse.
That which does not hold a
particular form
can enter even that which seems
impenetrable.
This is why we practice
"effortless effort."
We act without ado.
We teach without arguments.

This is the way of true happiness,
but because people prefer
distractions and noise,
it is not a popular way.

---

44. Stop Exhausting Ourselves

Is fame worth the sacrifice
of our true nature?
Does wealth compensate
for the loss of ourselves?
Which causes more suffering—
accumulating things,
or letting them all go?

Looking outside ourselves
for approval and security,
we find only suffering.
Understanding that we are capable
for our lives,
we stop exhausting ourselves
and begin enjoying ourselves.

---

45. Exactly What Is Needed

True perfection does not exhaust
itself
trying to appear perfect.
True abundance does not waste
itself
in showy displays.

The most direct path
will appear to wind about.
The greatest skill
will appear quite ordinary.
The most helpful words
will appear hesitant.

When we see clearly,
we act with tranquility,
and exactly what is needed is
done.

---

46. To Be Content with Each Breath

When we practice this path
our energy is focused on useful,
helpful tasks.
When we depart from this path,
fear contaminates our energy

and we become concerned with
self-protection.

Our greatest suffering comes
from not knowing who we are
or where we belong.
Our greatest unhappiness comes
from always wanting something
more,
something else.

To be content with each breath
is to be eternally content.
This is our practice.

---

47. Still We Accomplish Everything

It is not necessary to travel
to understand the world.
It is not necessary to look out the
window
to see into ourselves.

The more we look outside
ourselves for knowledge,
the less we know about anything.

We do not wander about
yet still we gain knowledge.
We do not look about
yet still we gain understanding.
We do not strive,
yet still we accomplish
everything.

---

48. . . . Until We Assume Nothing

Seeking knowledge,
we add new facts each day.
Seeking the Tao,
we drop assumptions each day.
Each day we assume less and less
until we assume nothing.
There is nothing left to do,
and nothing left undone.

Allowing things to come and go
according to their nature,
we gain everything.
Trying to control everything,
we gain nothing.

---

49. Open to the Hearts of All

We hold no fixed opinions.
Our hearts are therefore open
to the hearts of all.

We extend kindness to the kind
and unkind alike.
Thus kindness becomes our very
nature.

We extend trust to the trustworthy
and untrustworthy alike.
Thus trust becomes our very
nature.

We don't contend with people
by seeking to gain advantage.
People around us lose their edge

and we become loving friends
to the whole world.

50. Even Death Cannot Disturb Us

Life and death are inseparable.
One is form and the other is formless.
Each gives way to the other.
One-third of people concentrate on life
and ignore death.
One-third obsess over death
and ignore life.
One-third don't think of either
and just pass on through.
Each clings to conditioned ideas.
Each suffers.

Walking this path
we become skillful
at living without suffering.
We do not fear attack.
Therefore an attacker
has already lost the advantage.
Life and death have become the same;
therefore even death cannot disturb us.

51. Within the Heart of Every Being

The Tao expresses itself
in each and every being.
Its very presence nurtures us.
We are shaped and perfected by it
in the living of our lives.
Therefore each and every being honors the Tao
and delights in its presence,
not because they are commanded,
but because it is their nature.

We are expressions of the Tao.
Its presence sustains us,
develops us,
teaches us,
shelters us,
matures us,
and returns us to our origin.

The Tao gives us life
but does not claim to own us.
It is ever acting on our behalf
but expects nothing in return.
It is our true guide
but does not control us.

Its presence is deep within
the heart of every being.

52. Our Suffering Ends

The origin of all that is
can naturally be called "mother of all."
Finding our mother, we find our true self.
Finding our true self,
our suffering ends.

If we let our thoughts become still
and our needs become few,
we will live in peace.
If we follow our thoughts
and chase after distractions,
we will live in chaos.

Noticing small and ordinary things
is enlightenment.
Treating all beings with kindness
is strength.

Enlightenment is our natural
state.
Sitting in meditation we see our
hidden suffering,
accept it, lay it down,
and return to peace.

---

53. A Tiny Bit of Willingness

It takes just a tiny bit of
willingness
to follow this path,
but many things distract us.
This path is broad and steady
but we are conditioned to follow
our thoughts
down countless sidetracks.

Those who can afford distractions
gather them by the carload,
while the basic needs of most go
unmet.
The accumulation of luxuries
is contrary to this path.
It is a futile attempt to find
happiness by taking that
which is not freely given.

---

54. By Looking Within

If we establish ourselves on this
path,
we will not be shaken by events.
If we take it into our hearts,
our children and their children
will benefit.

This path returns us to our true
self.
It brings our families abundant joy.
It brings our communities a lasting
legacy.
It brings our countries true
prosperity.

All that is expresses this path.
Therefore we practice awareness
in each and every moment.
We see ourselves in every person
we meet.
The whole world becomes our
family,
our community,
our country.

How do we make this discovery?
By sitting still and looking within.

---

55. Natural Harmony

Embracing this path

we are like newborn children.
We are in natural harmony with all creatures,
bringing harm to none.
Our body is soft and flexible, yet strong.
Our vital passion is not limited
to sexual intercourse,
but empowers all of life.
Our harmony and focus allow us
to work all day at a single task
and not grow tired.

This harmony is experienced
only in the present moment.
It is in the present moment
that we see the way ahead.
Everything in life becomes a blessing.
Forcing events to be other than they are
only brings us misery.

---

56. The Treasure of Our Being

The more we understand this path,
the less we need to convince others.
The more we need to convince others,
the less we really understand.

So we become silent.
We stop looking about for approval.
We cease taking offense
at the opinions of others.
We no longer complicate our thinking
or our lives.
We do not seek the spotlight
but instead become a simple part of all that is.

We can be loved or shunned,
make a profit or suffer a loss,
be honored or disgraced,
and never lose the treasure of our being.

---

57. Let Life Live Itself

To guide a country
we use administrative skills.
To wage a war
we use surprise tactics.
But to gain joy in living
we let life live itself.

What does "let life live itself" mean?
The harder we try
the more our efforts fail.
The more we arm ourselves
the more chaos we experience.
The more schemes we plan
the less predictable are the results.
The more rules we impose
the more we become rule breakers.

So in this practice
we stop trying to change ourselves
and find that we naturally change.

We stop trying to be good
and find that goodness is our nature.
We stop trying to get rich,
and find that our life is full of abundance.

We stop trying to get our own way
and find that we enjoy our life.

---

58. This Path Is Unobtrusive

This path is unobtrusive,
allowing the simple purity
of those who follow it to emerge.
If it were a path of interference and control,
those who tried to follow it would be miserable
and would soon turn aside.

What we call good fortune and bad fortune
are mixed together in all events.
If we try to have one without the other,
we will become completely confused
and everyone's suffering will increase.

The one who follows this path
will have firm principles,
but will never impose them
or injure others in their name;
will be honest, but never cruel;
will be consistent,
but never at the expense of others;
will be a guide to people,
but never overshadow them.

---

59. Gentle Ease

Moderation is the best way
to care for our affairs.
It frees us from fixed plans
that waste our power.
We never punish ourselves
for things we do or don't do,
so our power remains available.
With it we can respond
to the shifting winds of life
and use everything for good.

We are able to take care of our affairs,
no matter how complicated,
with the gentle ease
of a mother caring for her child.

Deeply rooted in our practice,
we never become confused
or lose our way.

---

60. Transformed into Wisdom

We take care of our most important affairs
in the same way we fry a small fish.
We don't force the issue.
We don't hurry the process.

Our conditioned thoughts

of worry and of doubt
have lost their power.
We still notice them arising,
but they no longer run our lives.

Because we walk along this path,
that which used to make us suffer
has been transformed into
wisdom.

61. Everyone Is Welcome

A country centered in this path
is like a fertile valley.
All the world flows to it
and finds a place of rest and
welcome.
Its stillness and tranquility
overcome the restlessness
around it
and all find lasting peace.

This is our path of life.
We flourish not by pretending to
be grand,
but by making a welcoming space
for all.
When we bow a welcome to a
stranger,
the stranger becomes a friend.
When the stranger bows a welcome
in return,
we become a friend.
Everyone is welcome.
Everyone is home.

62. The Source of All That Is

This path is the source of all that is.
It is the refuge of those who
follow it.
It is the protector of those who
ignore it.

We honor those
who show no interest in this path
with gentle words and
loving-kindness.

Greater than any gift of wealth or
power
is the quiet offering of ourselves to
one another.
Two truths guide our practice:
"Look inside and you will find,"
and
"You are free of fault."

For this reason this path
is dear to us beyond all else.

63. For Ourselves and for All Beings

Action on this path unfolds
without effort.
Work is accomplished without
strain.
Life is enjoyed without clinging.
The smallest things are honored
and the greatest things are seen as
ordinary.
Ill treatment is seen

as an opportunity for kindness.
Small steps lead to great accomplishments.
Difficult tasks are seen
as a series of easy steps.
Therefore we pay complete attention
to the task in front of us.
There is no frivolous way to end our suffering.
By giving ourselves to the present moment,
this is exactly what we do,
for ourselves and for all beings.

---

64. The Single Small Step

Sitting still allows us to notice
the subtle stirrings of the mind.
Small thoughts that lead to suffering
are seen early and easily set aside.
Since trouble begins in the mind,
we watch the mind with care
and trouble is stopped before it begins.

This practice seems so passive and still.
Yet it is the seedling
from which the great tree grows.
It is the single small step
that begins the journey of a thousand miles.

If we hurry or force our practice,
it slips away from us.
We release ideas
of success and failure.
We patiently take the next necessary step
and everything unfolds as it should.
We lay down our wanting
and pick up our contentment.
We lay down our conditioning
and pick up our true nature.

We gently help all beings everywhere
return to their true nature.

---

65. Live in Fullness, Return in Joy

The great teachers of this path
taught with humble simplicity.
No cathedrals, no books, no ado at all.
Just one person talking to another
about ordinary life.

Today the experts babble
about everything under the sun,
seeking to gather crowds
and control circumstances by their clever words.
Everyone is cheated.

We are truly blessed only
by one who teaches
from the heart.

This one reveals
the secrets of the universe:
how all forms and all beings
express the power of the Tao
by the fullness of their life,
and then return to their source.
The heart of our teaching
is to live in fullness
and return in joy.

66. Great Is Their Honor

Streams and rivers carve ravines
and canyons
because they flow down to the
ocean.
The power is in the downward
flow.

One who helps us with this
practice
speaks and acts with humility.
Therefore our own power flows.
One who leads us on this path
follows along behind.
Therefore our own true nature
leads.

Our gratitude to the countless
beings
who have transmitted this path
down to the present day
is without limit.
They taught with gentleness and
grace.
Few of their names are known.
Great is their honor.

67. Compassion Is the Root

No one sees anything special about
this path.
Yet it is because it appears
ordinary
that it remains wondrous.
No one has been able to market it.
No one has trivialized it.

There are three virtues inherent in
this path:
compassion, simplicity, and
patience.
Wherever there is compassion,
fear does not abide.
Wherever there is simplicity,
generosity resides.
Wherever there is patience,
all things are accomplished.

If we try to be fearless
and do not have compassion,
we become ruthless.
If we try to be generous
and do not have simplicity,
we become controlling.
If we try to accomplish things
and do not have patience,
we become failures.

Compassion is the root of all these
virtues.
It is the very nature of the Tao.

It is the energy that binds all
things together.

—

68. Not Trying to Fix

When confrontation arises
we face it without aggression.
When someone opposes us
we do not give in to anger.
We view no one as a competitor
because we do not seek our
own way.

—

We know our strengths
and we know our weaknesses.
We use them each for benefit.
We are not trying to fix ourselves
or others
so we move naturally and easily
along our path.

—

69. Call No One Enemy

Military strategists agree.
They would rather defend
than make a foolish attack.
They would rather consolidate
than overextend.

—

So we move forward
without conquering anyone.
We gain
without anyone losing.
We confront obstacles
without using weapons.

—

We call no one enemy,
for to call someone enemy
is to lose our inner unity.
We become divided against
ourselves
and everyone suffers.

—

When conflict arises
we refuse to separate ourselves.
This is how we remain at peace.

—

70. Easy to Find and Follow

Our conditioned ways
of seeing things and doing things
make it hard for us to understand.
But this path is easy to find
and easy to follow.

—

This path arises from the source
of all.
Its power enlivens all things.
If we learn to know this source,
we learn to know ourselves.

—

Following this path we are led
to the inner treasure of our being.
Our outer trappings remain simple
so we are free to cherish our
inner joy.

—

71. We Know Its Ending

If we pretend to be aware
but do not recognize
our own suffering,
we remain ignorant.

—

The fundamental joy of this path is the awareness
of the suffering caused by our own mind.
Knowing its origin,
we know its ending.

72. Awe of the Mystery

If we have no awe of the mystery,
we are easily controlled by fear.
We constrict ourselves with self-hate
and become willing victims of other people.

Knowing our true nature,
we see ourselves clearly,
but do not become arrogant.
We cherish ourselves,
but not as separate from all other beings.
Our external identity
is nourished by our inner reality.

73. We Will Never Lose Our Way

We do the best we can
yet sometimes our actions seem harmful.
At other times
they seem beneficial.
We find no answer as to why this is so.
We are only shown the way to walk
one step at a time,
accepting both harm and benefit
as essential parts of life.
We are shown how to remain quiet
yet respond to every situation.
We are shown how to be present
even before we are called.
We are shown how to be patient
yet accomplish everything.

The mysteries and unknowns
along this path are many,
yet on it we will never lose our way.

74. We Will Surely Cut Ourselves

Our true nature does not fear death.
Our conditioned mind creates this fear
in a futile attempt to control events
and keep people in line.

Death is a natural part of this path.
An unnatural fear of death leads only to killing.
It is like trying to use the intricate tools
of a master craftsman.
We will surely cut ourselves.

75. Embrace True Simplicity

Why do the poor lack what they need?
Because the rich consume too much.

Why do people become restless
and discontent?
Because those in power try to
control
every aspect of their lives.

Everyone is so concerned
with getting and keeping
that no one learns to really live
before they die.

To follow this path
we must abandon overconsumption
and embrace true simplicity.

---

76. Our True Strength

Before we are conditioned
by all the "dos and don'ts" of life,
we are naturally tender and gentle.
As we grow old,
we constrict around these
conditions
and end up dying stiff and rigid.
Indeed all living things begin soft
and supple
and end up brittle and dry.

So we see that hardness and
inflexibility
are signs of death,
and that tenderness and gentleness
are signs of life.

It is the ability of an army to
change its plans
that keeps it from defeat.
It is the ability of a tree to bend in
the wind
that keeps it from toppling.
Our natural tenderness
is our true strength.

---

77. Dynamic Balance

Following this path is like
stringing a bow.
One end is pulled down
and the other is pulled up,
creating a dynamic balance.
So this practice encourages a
dynamic balance
between excess and deficiency.
When we see an excess,
we reduce it.
When we see a deficiency,
we give to it.

This is contrary to common
wisdom.
Common wisdom seeks
to constantly increase excess.
To do this, that which is lacking
must decrease even more.
Balance is destroyed.

To keep balance we must trust
this path
and keep to our true nature.
This allows us to give without
worry,
and to receive without attachment.

---

78. Soft and Yielding
This path seems paradoxical.
Like water, it is soft and yielding,
yet there is no better way to
overcome
the stiffness and rigidity
that causes so much suffering.

We intuitively know that flexibility
is more effective than stubbornness
and that tenderness is superior
to hard-heartedness,
yet our conditioned habits keep us
from acting on this knowledge.

By accepting all that seems humble
and plain,
we become masters of every
situation.
By opening our hearts
to all that seems painful and
difficult,
we help end all suffering.
No wonder it seems paradoxical.

---

79. No Special Favorites
Resentment always leads
to more resentment.
Only contentment leads
to contentment.
Therefore we do not seek advantage
or control.
Our contentment is independent
of the actions of others.
Seeking a special position
is not the way of life.

There are no "special favorites"
along this path.
It unfolds itself before whoever
walks along it.

---

80. We Have Truly Lived
The present moment is all we
have,
so we are not constantly seeking
a faster way to do things
or a better place to be.
Our vehicles sit idle except when
truly needed,
and our weapons remain locked
away.

Our attention is always on
the experience of the moment
so we enjoy our food,
our clothing,
our homes,
and every aspect
of a simple way of living.

Though the world is filled
with sights we haven't seen,
we die content because
we have truly lived.

---

81. We Always Have Enough
The most helpful words
do not please our conditioning.

Words that please our conditioning
are not helpful.
This path is not taught by
argument.
Those who argue are not
teaching this path.
Books cannot teach this path.
If we rely on books
we will not find this path.

Simplicity is our joyous and
practical guide.
Therefore we always have enough
to live with generosity.
In this way our path brings
great gain
yet does no harm.
No longer striving for control,
we discover life to be an
ever-flowing river.

Acknowledgments

With gratitude for the wisdom and poetry of Lao-Tzu.

With gratitude for Alan Watts, who introduced me to the Tao.

With gratitude for Chungliang Huang, who taught me to dance the Tao.

With gratitude for Gwen Hawkes, my editor at Hachette Books, whose encouragement kept me at it, and who saved me from the depths of proof editing.

About the Author

William Martin is the author of many books that explore the applications of Taoism to modern life, including the popular *The Parent's Tao Te Ching* and *A Path and a Practice*. He is a graduate of the University of California at Berkeley and of Western Theological Seminary in Holland, Michigan.

In his own words he describes his path as "a winding one that has taken me through roles as a scientist, a minister, a psychotherapist, a college instructor, a Taoist teacher, and an author. It has led me to explore beliefs and ways of living that include Zen Buddhism, Christianity, and Taoism.

"I have lived in cities and towns and in the countryside. I have run marathons, walked in the desert, hiked up mountains and through forests, and I have found great beauty in the practice of Tai Chi and Qigong. For more than forty years, I have translated, written about, and pondered the Tao Te Ching. Today, I live with my wife, Nancy, in the Sonoran desert of southern Arizona where the stark beauty of this landscape deeply nurtures our souls."

Bill continues to teach Taoist thought and Qigong to individuals and groups through his website: https://www.williammartin.org.